Magical Oils
by Moonlight

- Understand Essential Oils,
  Their Blends and Uses
- Discover the Power of the Moon Phases
- Learn the Meanings of Oils
- Choose the Appropriate Day and Time

By
MAYA HEATH

This edition first published in 2004 by New Page Books, an imprint of
Red Wheel/Weiser, LLC
With offices at:
65 Parker Street, Suite 7
Newburyport, MA 01950
www.redwheelweiser.com
www.newpagebooks.com

ISBN: 978-1-56414-733-2
Library of Congress Cataloging-in-Publication Data
Heath, Maya, 1948-
    Magical oils by moonlight : understand essential oils, their blends and uses;
    discover the power of the moon phases; learn the meanings of oils; choose the
    appropriate day and time / by Maya Heath.
        p. cm.
    Includes index.
    ISBN 1-56414-733-9 (pbk.)
     1. Essences and essential oils—Miscellanea. 2. Moon—Phases—Miscellanea.
    3. Magic. I. Title.

BF1442.E77H43 2004
133.4'3--dc22

2003070211

Cover design by Cheryl Cohan Finbow
Cover and interior illustrations by Maya Heath
Interior by Kristen Parkes

Printed in the United States of America
IBI
10 9 8 7 6 5 4 3 2 1

To Phillip, companion of my heart, for his patience, love,

and support in all the parts of my life.

Acknowledgments

Regardless of the name on the title page, a book is the work of many. The teachers who have guided us along the way, the friends and family who love and encourage us, and the editors and production staff that bring a work into reality all have their imprint on the finished work. While specific thanks would fill a volume themselves, there are a few who should be especially mentioned for their help and support through this process. My thanks to Steve Pitt for his advice with the color and tone correspondences and for his friendship and help on many levels. Thank you to friends Pam Steele, Susan Jackson, Tammi Johnson, and Trish Telesco. Taking the step from author to illustrator was much due to their continued faith and encouragement. Great gratitude goes to my daughter, Phoenix, for cheerfully turning the wheels of life while this work was being written and illustrated, for patiently modeling for some of the figure drawings, and for reminding me that life is more than work, and insisting that every once in a while, at least a day out together is one of life's most precious treasures and, actually, the reason for all the work. What is life if you don't enjoy it? And very, very high on my list of gratitude are Wade and Dianne Berlin. Their love and support over the years has been invaluable to my life and my creative endeavors. Their continued friendship is a joy. And my great thanks go to Don and Ruth Montgomery for the shelter of their home, their encouragement, and the delight of their company.

Contents

Preface

I cannot remember a time when I was not fascinated with the world of the unseen. I remember as a child seeing astrological symbols on someone's charm bracelet and being intrigued by the idea of the secrets they might hold. As I grew up, I explored world mythology and ancient civilizations. I was struck with the power of the art that all peoples throughout time have created to try and communicate their relationship with Divine beings and their own inner spiritual awareness. And so art, Spirit, and magic became entwined in my universe. I have been privileged to have some wonderful opportunities of study and fine teachers in my life as I searched out the pieces of how these three concepts related to one another. I was fortunate enough to be living in Houston at a time when the whole field of magic, metaphysics, and witchcraft was opening up. I studied traditional witchcraft with a student of Sybil Leek's, caballah with Ophiel, meditation and breathing techniques with William David, and metaphysics with the Theosophical Society. I was exposed to yoga and Silva Mind Control. In following these many threads, I found as many commonalities as differences, and built the intellectual groundwork that enabled a lifetime of study and investigation.

This work is very much the product of those studies and a lifetime of working with the knowledge gained. New methods that have come on the horizon have only served to strengthen practices rooted in ancient history. As life and study progress, the boundaries between the natural world of Earth and the celestial world of Spirit dissolve to reveal a fascinating whole. Symbols common to alchemists describe the modern world of physics and magic. The power of the Moon and the seasons of the year mark not only the cycles of the physical Earth, but cycles of Universal Energy, as well as the inner cycles of human lives and consciousness. Over the years I have observed the effects of the Moon cycles on my garden, on my pets, and on human beings. From a basis in traditional herbal magic, I branched into the powers of essential oils and found that the palette of potential expanded enormously with their concentrated powers. All of this has culminated in this present work—a view of the magical world seen as a continuum—the world of inner awareness seen as part and parcel of the Universal Energies that drive daily life. What I present here to you is the world of magic as it has revealed itself to me through a lifetime of study in the hope that it will provide a basis for your own research and study. I hope that this will form a beginning for you to explore the universe of magic and mystery that surrounds us in every moment—waking and sleeping—with every breath we take.

I believe that magic is here for everyone and is right at our fingertips. Whether people are looking for personal inner awakening, the key to their innate intuitive abilities, or the power to transform their lives and surroundings, the books I write are intended to help open those doors for people. We live in a wonderful world of energy and Spirit. It's here for everyone to celebrate. I wish you the joy of the journey.

The Act of Creating Reality

Introduction

As human beings, we possess a dual awareness. We are creatures of this physical world living day to day with its particular selection of goals, freedoms, and barriers. The vehicle that carries us—the physical body—evolved in the primordial seas from the first single-celled life forms, just as all living creatures around us did. We are also spirits manifesting in the physical world, formed from the stuff of stars and the Greater Universe, consciously interacting with the physical Universe through the vehicle of the physical body. It is our consciousness of this dual nature that sets us apart from the rest of Creation and it is what gives us the individual determinism with which to steer our lives through choice and action. In all of our daily existence, we are constantly involved in manipulating the parameters of our existence to achieve our purposes. We find goals we wish to achieve and then we move to extend our freedoms and reduce our barriers so that we can reach them. Not only is this a course of mundane action, it is a course of will and intention. It is our will that defines our world as surely as any physical circumstances that we are likely to encounter.

Magic is an act of will, manifesting itself across energy planes of reality to bring forth a creation of circumstance—to achieve the determined goal. To make the most of that act of will, we need to make the most of all the tools available to us as creatures of both flesh and Spirit. It is only by bridging the gap between the two that we create the path by which we bring our dreams into reality. The creation of that bridge is an act of personal transformation—an internal process to generate external results. It is a process to align our energies and intention with the energy structure of the world in which we intend to manifest that creation. This is a process that demands inner discipline and focus, as well as intelligent study of the elements we wish to manipulate. By doing this, we find ways to adjust our own inner energies of mind, emotions, body, and spirit to coincide with the energy currents of the larger world, and through a concerted act of will, bring our intentions into concrete reality. By aligning ourselves with the subtle energies that surround us and comprise the physical world, we create a bridge from the unseen to the seen—from potential to reality.

Because it is into this world that we wish to bring the reality of our will and the place where our goals will be played out and achieved, we use the tools that it presents to us. The seasons, the Moon's changing faces, and the physical elements are the stuff with which we draw the object of our will. Our inner power is always there—unchanging and unique—but by utilizing the forces of the physical, we make our work much easier and much more likely to achieve the results we desire. Even though we may be strong swimmers, it is far more likely that we will reach our destination if we swim with the tide rather than against it. And it is by observing the natural world that is intimately in tune with these forces that we take our cue to what these forces may be. As beings of mortal flesh, we are creatures of those same forces as the world we seek to manipulate. Magic is about changing ourselves so that what we wish is drawn to us. No matter what the purpose of the work, it requires a process of personal development to allow the individual to be receptive to the results. It is through the combined actions of inner change and outer alignment that we create our world and the circumstances that come to us.

Our bodies and our lives are made from the elements that also make up the stars. We are integrally connected to all things animate and inanimate by our kinship with the elements. The same atoms that make the earth and heavens make us as well. Our spirits are made from the same structured consciousness that weaves through every atom and current of energy that animates Creation in this Universe, as well as all the higher planes to which it is connected. The smallest drop of sea spray contains all the elements of the entire ocean from its deepest depths to the sparkling wave from which it is thrown. Every element that exists in the Universe exists in us as well. Every quality and potential we can conceive of exists within us, and although we may feel that it is lacking in our lives or beyond us, it requires only an act of alignment to bring it forth into our lives. Through magic, we focus on that universal connection to find the links within our own consciousness that will bring what we desire into manifestation. It is ours already; we have only to realize it. To this end we create a ritual format, constructing a model of the energy pattern of our purpose. Assembled from daily objects at hand, this ritual gives those objects special significance and energy, setting them in a framework that provides a focal point for our focused will and a central point from which we gain our connection with what we desire.

Defining the Purpose

The most important part of all and the first step of any work is deciding what you want. Vague wishes and goals will only get you vague results at best. And launching fuzzy expectations out into the void will probably get you nothing. Like an arrow notched into a bowstring, your goal must be straight and to the point. Thoughts have power of their own in a very real sense. Even in the study of physics, scientists are discovering that certain subatomic particles will behave the way they are expected to rather than in a mechanistic, predictable pattern that can be objectively analyzed. Photons will move in the direction researchers want them to under certain conditions. Even in the lofty halls of academia and research, pragmatic science is beginning to recognize that the boundaries between thought and reality are blurred. Every time you make an inner statement, the Universe is moved to comply in agreement. It is all well and good to say that we want "life to be better," but that implies a wide range of potential circumstances as well as an infinitely variable timeline. Saying to yourself *I want to be happy* may not work at all if it is followed up with the thought *but I don't deserve it*, even in the private corners of your mind. Every day we make inner decisions about our lives, and especially about our relationship to what our lives bring us. Living is a moment-to-moment act of creation.

Every act of conscious will and magic must contain at least a momentary foray into the realm of self-analysis as you determine what, exactly, it is that you really want to achieve. To say, "I want to be loved," or some such similar statement, is not enough. Do you want to get lucky, to have a good time, to have the delirious rush of being in love, or a lifetime commitment? These are all very different and require some selectivity. Once you have identified what your goal really is, the next step is to find within yourself not only what external circumstances are barring you from achieving it, but what inner motivations are holding the lack of it in place. Inner honesty is essential before any real work can begin. No matter how elaborate and well-planned your work is, you will never achieve the results you want if you are following it up with self-doubt and denial.

It should also be said that the most profound magical work you ever do will not succeed unless you follow it up with some real-world action. Wanting to be loved, no matter how specifically you define it, is only the first step, and will go nowhere unless you go out of your front door, make yourself personable, and meet people. Wanting a better job is only the first step that must be followed by the specific action of applying for that better job. Magic can put the cycles of time and energy at your disposal to make all things favorable for achievement, but you must take the steps necessary in order to finalize its process into manifestation.

Freedoms and Barriers

Part of your analysis of the situation should be an in-depth look at the barriers standing between you and your goal. It is quite possible that you need other things to happen before your process can be complete. You may want to be a brain surgeon, but that will not happen unless you go to medical school first. Setting out a plan of steps to achieve what you want may be next in the order of your work after clarifying your purpose. Consequently, it is always profitable to take a few steps back from what you perceive your goal to be and decide whether you should work through a series of preparatory steps towards its achievement.

One of the most insidious barriers to achieving your goal is you, yourself. Your own attitudes and hidden considerations on any given subject can cause you to shoot yourself down before you even get off the runway. All of us have a dark closet of self-doubt and belief in our own limitations. The Universe is impartial and will listen to these thoughts with the same attention to detail as it hears and responds to any others. Magic is also a process of confronting and dealing with these negative, limiting images in preparation to the final affirmation of your desire. It may be no easy thing to delve into these darker regions of your heart and mind, but without doing so, any work you do is likely to be considerably less effective.

This is why we follow the transitional elements of the cycle of the Moon. There are times and seasons of nature when the natural currents of energy are most favorable to looking inward in order to reveal and eliminate these negative influences, whether these forces are external ones or ones we carry inside us. Dark times provide the best energy for dealing with the limitations of your life and Spirit. They encourage a climate of inner critical honesty and action that can prepare the ground for sowing the seeds of change. Magical work that provides a truly lasting change of circumstances often requires that you move through these preparatory phases first. Like the tides of the ocean, they flush the waters of the Spirit, taking out the stagnant waters and trash of our consciousness while bringing fresh energies, ripe with possibility. And like the active process of the tides, you must be prepared to be proactive and deal with what you find in your analysis. It will do no good to discover powerful limiting forces working in your life if you then choose to ignore them or convince yourself you are powerless against them. The darker times of the Moon favor removal of these elements. Whether they are inner forces or external ones, you must act for their removal or containment so they will not compromise the work you are doing for change.

Generally speaking, when dealing with barriers, you will find they come in three ways, which will indicate the elements of the spell you want to take care of: (1) removal of the source of the problem, (2) removal of the effects of that source, and (3) ways to keep the problem from reoccurring. Depending on the severity of the issue of the problem, it might be wise to do each of these elements in a separate step of your work.

Along with the barriers to achievement, there are also freedoms. These are assets, talents, attitudes, strengths, and resources that will help you on your way. Perversely, these are often ignored because the focus is on what you do not have. Any analysis you do of your situation should include an equally critical look at where your freedoms lie. Often, once you deal with the barriers you are facing, you can get a fresh, positive look at where your strong points lie. You must actively cultivate these things as well. It will do you no good to acknowledge you have beautiful hair if you do not wash and comb it. Part of your magical process should always include a focus on these inner and outer abilities so that you can weave them into the work you are doing. Just as the Moon's dark times encourage removal and clearing out, the brightening times give you the energies necessary to optimize your strengths and turn the tides in your favor.

Taking the celestial timing a step further, there are more subtle seasons of the stars' cycles that can further qualify the Moon's energy and make it an even more powerful element in your process of inner change and alignment. As the Moon moves through the heavens, it crosses the area of the sky that is occupied by each of the signs of the zodiac. As it does so, its energy takes on the quality of the sign, making its energy more specific to the purpose. The stars are also said to influence, or "rule over," the elements you will be using in your physical ritual work. When all these things are taken into account and aligned with the purpose, your chosen goal, it is possible to use these currents of energy to your advantage to make the work both easier and more powerful.

Tools for Change

Chapter 1

Science tells us that our sense of smell is the only one of our senses whose sensory messages do not go through the rational part of our brain. Instead, it connects directly with instinctive and unconscious behavior. This poses an argument that it was the first sense to be developed in the course of evolution. We retain the complexity for thought or reason from a time before our brains developed, when life manifested as simple organisms cognizant only of the air or water in which they lived. The sense of smell is primal and basic to all the other more refined senses and doubtless was retained in the course of our evolution as a first line of response. Smell keys us to survival—to eating, mating, and the relative safety or danger of our surroundings.

The action of smelling something bypasses our conscious mind and addresses itself directly to our instincts by causing minute changes in our brain chemistry that, in turn, send signals directly to our automatic responses. Nerves, muscles, and internal organs—all these systems respond to these signals, changing our tone and response to our environment before we have even consciously thought about it. To test this theory, just imagine the smell of baking cookies. At just the thought, many people smile and subtly relax. Now imagine the smell of something rotten in the trash. Without thinking about it, the face changes and the body tenses.

By using specific scents we can intentionally address the body's physical, mental, and emotional responses. This practice is called aromatherapy. It is the study of how different smells affect the body, mind, emotions, and Spirit by using the distilled extracts of plants, flowers, and herbs. Human beings have been doing this for as long as history has been recorded. Perfumes are some of the most ancient means of adornment and making us more attractive to one another. Perfumes and incense have also been used for thousands of years in the practice of magic and religion because they help attune the individual to the vibrations of the powerful but unseen Greater Universe. Because our sense of smell directly addresses the body's chemistry and nervous responses, we can use it to attune ourselves to the subtle vibrations of the unseen world.

Emotions, thoughts, and physical responses are all basically energy. Their physical seat resides in our brain. Their combined energy patterns describe "where" we are in the Universe. They locate us in terms of our response to the world around us; they are also the means by which we create our reality. By changing brain chemistry we are literally changing our energy structure and our potential for alignment with other energy structures—specifically the energy structure of our goal. The scent pattern you use in your work will be the single most important tool in structuring the changes you wish to bring about.

Essential oils and oil blends are the basic ingredients. They are called oils because they are not soluble in water. The term *essential* is used because the word comes from the Latin *essentia*, meaning a liquid that is sufficiently volatile that it becomes a gas. They are also sometimes referred to as volatile oils, coming from the Latin word *volare*, meaning to fly. Old apothecaries called them "spirits," as in "Spirits of Turpentine," meaning essential oil of pine. In German they are referred to as *astherische ole*, which means ethereal oils. All these refer to their quality of being perceived and valued not in their liquid form, but in their gaseous one. These oils are extracted from plants and can come from any one or a combination of the plants' parts— petals, stems, leaves, bark, roots, or resins—by a variety of processes such as pressing, distillation, or chemical extraction. Their quality and purity can also vary depending on the process and the parts of the plants used. Their prices can vary depending on the complexity of the process and the amount of raw material necessary to extract a usable quantity of oil. Some essences require thousands of pounds of flower petals to render a single dram of oil.

Because some essences are so expensive or rare, modern chemistry has found ways to synthesize their scent. Sometimes combinations of other flowers are used that simulate the fragrance of a more expensive one. Other times, chemicals are blended that counterfeit an essence altogether. It is tempting to use these cheaper chemical oils because of their reasonable price and availability. However, although their smell may fool an inexperienced nose, their chemical composition will not fool the brain and subtler instincts. When dealing with energy, it is always better to use as close to the real thing as possible, balancing price with function. The results will speak for themselves.

Using Scent in Your Work

The blend of oils you make to suit your purpose is the central element that will bind all the others together. So to speak, it is the train of thought that carries you through from conception to manifestation. It will be used by itself on your skin and clothing, and in combination with other ingredients to make the incense and bath salts. You will use it to charge candles and anoint the objects and tools you use. It will be carried with you in a scent bag or misted in your space with an atomizer. Because of this, it is important to select the scent or blend of scents carefully, as this will set the tone for all the rest of your work. By themselves, oil blends can be used directly on the body like perfumes, although it is wise to do a skin test before you actually begin your work to make sure you do not have an allergic reaction to them. Because they are highly concentrated, they have the potential to irritate the skin.

Taking your time to choose wisely and blend carefully can be an important part of the work that you do. The formulae that are used as examples here are meant to be just that—examples. The list of oils available on the market is long and varied, giving you a wide range from which to pick and choose. If a particular scent offends you or causes an allergic reaction, there are others you may replace it with, but adjust the other oils to match it. Ideally, the formula that you use should be one of your own devising. Nothing can be more personal than what you make yourself from the wellspring of your own creativity. Nothing can match your desire more specifically.

Blending oils is an art that may take some practice and experimentation. Your magical working contains more than a single thought; it is a combination of ideas, needs, and wishes. Just so, the oil you blend should carry this through. It should combine properties that represent the elements or ideas of your wish that also harmonize well together as a scent. When blending oils from a recipe or when writing down a recipe that you have formulated, it is important to remember that the order in which you mix them is as important as the oils themselves or their proportion of the mixture. Changing the order in which the oils are mixed changes the way they combine chemically, and the scent will be noticeably different. So, as you work, follow the recipe exactly. If you are blending your own, record what you are doing. Write it down as you go rather than trying to remember later what you did.

Advice on Your Choice of Oils

At the end of the book are two appendices of charts of essences categorized by both function and oil name. You will notice that there are a lot of different scents listed in each category. This is not a suggestion to use all the essences listed. Besides being unnecessarily expensive, the resulting concoction would probably smell terrible. Also, availability of essences varies widely from place to place, as do prices and qualities. The extensive list is provided to give you choices. For example, if you hate the smell of cinnamon or if jasmine makes you sneeze, you do not need to use them. You may select an alternative from the list that will suit your purpose just as well. Each section will have guidelines for making basic oil blends as well as some time-tested recipes. This book is intended to give you the information and basis to develop your own blends that are specific to your needs and your own way of working. Consequently, the lists include many ingredients that are unusual, as well as the more basic scents that are commonly found.

There are also some basic ideas from the area of perfumery it is helpful to consider. Fragrances can be divided into nine categories based on the fundamental nature of the scent. These divisions are not hard-and-fast classifications and many times perfumers differ as to which categories certain scents are assigned.

- **Flowery:** Jasmine, rose, honeysuckle, lily of the valley, violet, lilac, tuberose, magnolia, orange blossom.
- **Fruity:** Plum, pineapple, peach, raspberry, apple, mandarin.
- **Oriental:** Frankincense, myrrh, spikenard, opium.
- **Amber:** Amber, vanilla, balsam.
- **Spicy:** Cinnamon, ginger, clove, nutmeg, coriander, cardamom.

- **Woodsy/Mossy:** Pine, lavender, fir, rosemary, oakmoss, patchouli, redwood.
- **Animal** (long-lasting and permeating): Besides being expensive, the derivation of these oils comes from the glands of animals. In the interest of kindness to animals and conservation of life, synthetic reproductions of these essences should be used. Ambergris (sperm whale), deer musk, civet musk, castoreum (beaver).
- **Citrus:** These are bright and invigorating but tend to be of short duration. Bergamot, citrus fruit such as lemon, lime, orange, tangerine.
- **Green** (bright and enlivening): Like the citrus, they tend to be of short duration. Mown grass, warm sunlit meadows, grasses, leaves, ivy, basil, chamomile.

When blending a scent, perfumers describe the formula in terms of a musical chord describing the way in which a blend presents itself and develops as it is used. When blending a fragrance intended to be worn, it is a good idea to keep some of these guidelines in mind. If you work with the oil lists at the end of each section, you can find scents that fall into each category that suit the purpose of your wish spell. With a little practice and experimentation, you will be able to assemble a group of scents that not only works magically, but also pleases the senses. Ideally, the proportions should be that the combined amounts of the heart (middle) and base notes equal the top note. This is not a hard-and-fast rule, however, and each should be evaluated by the nature and strength of the oils you are using as well as the purpose you have in mind for it. For instance, allspice is particularly potent and a little goes a very long way, and even a little can overpower a blend. Approach it drop by drop until you have just enough. Let your nose be your ultimate guide.

Top Note

The first impression of a fragrance lasting less than a minute—citrus, green, delicate floral.

In magic, this is the note that opens the way for the others to follow, setting the theme for the heavier work of the stronger scents—it represents the main reason for which you are doing the work.

Heart Note

The second level that develops as the fragrance warms with the skin—often it is made of warm woods—sandalwood, vanilla, cedar, vetivert, balsam, frankincense, benzoin. This represents the emotional element of your work and that connects your will to the higher planes of working.

Base Note

The final scent that develops as the fragrance interacts with the skin chemistry.

This defines the basic purpose and power of what you desire. It is the unifying force that ultimately leads to manifestation.

Storing Your Blend

Essential oils are volatile natural products, and, as such, are sensitive to sunlight and extreme temperatures. Once you have made your blend, it is important to store it properly so that its properties remain potent. Use clean, new glass bottles with tightly fitting lids. You can usually buy these at the same place you purchase the essential oils. If possible, the glass should be colored—amber or green is a good choice. If you wish to take this a step further, you might be able to find glass bottles that are the color of the energy that best describes your formula (Chapter 8) or the planetary energy under which you are working (Chapter 7). Whatever color glass you choose, the finished product should be stored in a cool, dark place. A closed box or cupboard is a good choice. **Never** use plastic containers to store your basic blend. The chemical substances in the oil are likely to react with the plastic container and spoil both the oil and the container. If you are making a spray mist, find a glass spray bottle and do not plan on using the container for long-term storage because the moving parts of the sprayer are plastic.

The Doing and the Becoming

The goal of your work will determine the timing of your work. It will also determine the oil blend you use. When these basic steps are in place, it will be the time to assemble the physical elements of your spell in order to set up a ritual space that will be the actual focal point of the spell. They will be representative of the five metaphysical elements that make up our physical world because this is the world in which you intend to manifest your work.

Each of these steps is important and relevant to the work you are doing. The action of performing the spell will set the wheels of change in motion. Just as important as it is to do the preparatory work carefully, it is important to be prepared to follow it with action in the Universe. Be aware of the changes as they come to you. Unlike the fantasy movies and television where the results appear in a flash of green smoke, the physical Universe obeys its own laws. Indeed, nothing can exist or occur in any Universe that goes contrary to its laws. Consequently, the results of your process will appear in real but sometimes subtle ways. Each time you act on those changes, you bring your goal closer to reality. But most important of all, you must know that what you are doing is real. It is your certainty of that reality that makes the final gateway from the *possible* to the *actual*. You have the tools of creation at your disposal; it rests within you to use them to change your world.

Planting Your Life by the Moon— The Times of Change

As modern human beings, many of us have come to live in cities, in buildings where we are constantly submerged in climate-controlled environments geared for our comfort. Although this has paved the way for greater productivity and greatly lengthened and enhanced lives, it has also served to distance us from our awareness of the natural world. Many of us have forgotten that as a species, we evolved as creatures of that natural world as much as any of the plants and animals with whom we share this planet. Far beyond the long cycle of birth, growth, aging, and death, we are governed by other cycles that subtly influence our living and consciousness. But even though these are obvious changes in the demands and energies of the year, our awareness of cycles and changes has become blunted by the enforced regularity of our lives.

In Spring, it is common to mention "Spring Fever" when referring to that inner restlessness we feel as we look out of the windows of our schools and offices. We feel a quickening of our pulses and a desire to run free in the fresh air. Summer brings a further burst of energy, urging us outdoors for physical work and play (until the intense heat of the dog days drives us back to the comfort of air conditioning). Fall brings its own inner season of introspection and a little melancholy as we store the lawn furniture and prepare for Winter's onslaught, moving our lives indoors to celebrate more somber holidays such as Halloween and, later, Thanksgiving. As Winter closes in, our moods withdraw as well, and our physical rhythms slow in response to colder temperatures and decreasing sunlight.

But there are shorter cycles still. The monthly cycles of the lunar rhythms are easy to miss as we regulate our patterns of activity and sleep with the aid of artificial lighting and television entertainment. But whether we choose to acknowledge or be aware of these natural clocks, we are inescapably the product of the same evolutionary cycles that brought us from single-celled organism to upright primate. The Moon that pulls the ocean's tides pulls our inner tides as well.

It has long been something of a debate among the noted authorities whether or not the Moon really has an effect on the behavior of humans and animals. Statisticians and psychologists may debate and deny that there is a correlation, but ask any bartender, firefighter, or emergency room attendant about the power of the Full Moon and you will have your observation by the experts that really matter. Year after year, almanacs are filled with sage advice on how to get the most out of the fruits and flowers in the garden by planting and tending them at the appropriate times. Life on Earth evolved from microorganisms in the ancient seas—and these microorganisms were mostly water. Although life forms became increasingly complex in their specialized functions, they still retained a large proportion of water in their structure. The Moon's magnetic force pulls at this water within— the blood in our bodies and the vital essences of plants—just as it pulls the great tides of the sea. We are attuned to our smallest fiber to the forces that move the planet and the stars.

As the Moon passes through its phases, the quality of this force differs both in strength and content. By observing its effects on the natural world, and on plants in particular, we can draw certain conclusions about how its force will affect other more subtle areas of our lives. As with gardening, each phase of the Moon has its proper set of activities. By planning our spiritual and magical workings around the energy of this powerful natural force, we can make the most of its influence while avoiding energies that might be counterproductive to the purpose at hand.

All crops that produce their yield above ground should be planted during the Waxing (New to Full) Moon; the first week is especially good for crops that have their seeds on the outside, such as asparagus, cabbage, broccoli, celery, and spinach. The second week (between the first quarter and the Full Moon) is best for crops that produce seeds on the inside, such as peppers, tomatoes, peaches, cucumbers, and melons. During the Waning Moon (Full to New Moon), plant root crops, such as potatoes, peanuts, carrots, and onions. This is the time to remove weeds from your garden or harvest crops that you plan to plow under. It is generally not considered wise to plant on the day of the New Moon.

Using this same logic, we can time the planting of more subtle seeds born of our wishes, will, and intentions. Just as the Moon's tidal pull varies the energy within the Earth and within the living cells of the plants in the garden, it also affects us mentally, emotionally, and physically to vary the strength and focus of our inner energies. By carefully choosing the time we set events in motion, we can make the most of the lunar power and greatly enhance the power of our work and its subsequent results.

The Moon cycles through its phases approximately every 28 days, giving us 13 lunar months to a 365-day solar year. Each of the phases, therefore, lasts about a week, with the most intense level of that particular energy being on the specific day of the cycle but extending one day on either side. This gives us a three-day window of opportunity for working in a particular phase. For example, work done for the Full and Dark of the Moon can be done with three-day candles (the ones in the jars about the size of a large juice glass) or can be started the day before the specific phase with the intention of having the work continue through the following day.

The first step of your process is to choose the appropriate time to work. Aligning your own power with natural ones will give your work that extra force needed to bring your plans forward to fruition.

Chapter 2

As the Moon grows smaller, its energy becomes negative and contracting. This is a time of preparation. As in gardening, the space must be cleared, old growth removed, and the earth tilled and broken up to make way for the seeds that you wish to plant and the seedlings that will later sprout. This is the time to work for the removal of things from your life by working with the energy of limiting and binding. Farmers have long known that this is the time to cut back or dig up vines and weeds so they will not come back from the roots. It is the time to plant root crops, that is, plants that will bear their fruits underground, and the same could be said for people and situations in your life. There is a principal issue here that many people ignore when doing work of preparation and clearing. When you engage in work to remove something from your life, you must be willing to let it go. The farmer clearing his garden from choking growth does not keep the weeds around for later just in case he needs something to fill a bare spot. He realizes that they will only choke any new productive crop that he plans to plant. So, hopefully, he gets rid of them entirely.

The same thing works in the case of problems. You must be willing to let go of them, to release the energy, the content, and the attachment. You cannot release a harmful person from your life and still plan to get back at them later. You cannot get rid of an unwanted suitor while wanting them to hang around just in case you need someone to go to the movies with next week. You cannot get a new job without leaving the old one. You cannot get rid of old habit patterns and still have them around just in case you don't find any new ones that you like. Once done is done; gone is gone.

This is an ancient principle called "sacrifice." The idea is that in order for a new and desired result to come into your life, you must make a space for it by "offering up" what is filling its spot. So the Waning Moon is the time when the energies are the most conducive to ridding yourself of things that you don't want in your life that are taking the place of things you do want. Just as the farmer, you are preparing the ground so that what you plant will bear the desired fruits. You are making space in the garden of your life.

A Safe and Peaceful Place

When you move into a new space, it is often a pleasant thing to not only clean it before you move your things in physically, but also to cleanse the atmosphere of previous tenants. You probably would not wear someone else's clothes without washing them first, and cleansing a place is part of this same idea. Whether you plan to follow this process with a full blessing ritual is up to you, but a brief cleansing is a good way to "push the reset button" and make a place truly your own. Also, in the process of living you are likely to go through difficult and unpleasant periods. The energy of your passages collects in your surroundings and environment. Just as you clean your house from time to time to get rid of the dust and dirt, it is a good idea to clean your personal energy space. New conditions are more easily brought about when the space is clean and refreshed. Old negative patterns are likely to perpetuate themselves. So whether your space is new or old, taking the time to cleanse and recharge a space can be a good step in your magical process.

Protective Herbs From the New World

Smudging is a general term used to describe filling an area with thick, aromatic smoke. It works to change the atmosphere of a person or place by not only making a pleasing scent to drive out less pleasant odors, it also works because the physical ions of the smoke bond with negatively charged energies in the environment to bind them and change them into more positive energies.

One of the most common combinations of herbs used for smudging comes from the New World—sage, sweetgrass, cedar, and copal.

A common way to use them is to put them into a smudge stick. A smudge stick is a bundle of herbs that has been bound together with a light string. The end or the bundle is held over a flame, such as a candle or oil lamp, until it starts to burn. Once it lights, blow gently on it until the flame goes out and only the glowing ember remains. Then you can either wave it in the air to make it smoke, or you can blow on it again to make the smoke thicker. Be sure that while you are doing this you hold the smudge stick over a fireproof dish or seashell, because it is likely to drop small sparks as it burns, which can damage the floor or carpet.

The most popular of these herbs is **white sage**. Sage is strongly purifying because it completely removes any previous energies from the environment and leaves you with a clean and open field on which you may charge your own intentions. The active property of the sage smoke is to de-ionize the atmosphere. That means that, on an atomic level, the sage smoke literally hooks itself onto discordant vibrations and neutralizes them by resetting their "charge" to zero. If you prefer, you can use a single leaf of sage. It works in the same way you would light a stick of incense by holding it to a flame first then blowing the flame out to leave a glowing ember. Take a small leaf of white sage and light it with a flame. Then blow it out, leaving the edge smoldering. Holding it over a shell or other fireproof plate or container, walk around the room(s) you wish to cleanse, blowing gently on the leaf so that the smoke flows into all the nooks and crannies.

Sweetgrass works in a very similar way to sage except that its action is gentler and more subtle. Instead of bound bundles or single leaves, sweetgrass is generally found in braids. Light one end of the braid until it smolders and, holding it over a fireproof container or shell, blow its smoke around your space. Sweetgrass sweetens not only the air, but the quality of the space. Its energy encourages lightness of heart and a reasonable balance and calm in the atmosphere.

You can also mix cedar leaves into sage leaves and sprinkle them over a glowing charcoal block if you prefer. This is specifically **flat leafed cedar**, not shavings of the wood. The cedar added to the sage will fortify it with a feeling of richness and well-being. Cedar is sometimes thought to encourage prosperity and confidence as well as encourage healing, protection, and purification. **Copal** is another ingredient that can be added to the smudge for purification. It also has the benefit of strengthening the heart center and, consequently, is effective when working in a bedroom where the occupant is having bad dreams or problems with anxiety of any kind. Unlike cedar, sage, or sweetgrass, copal is a resin that originally came from South America and looks similar to myrrh or frankincense beads. It is bought in chunks and is bound inside the bundle when the herbs are dried.

If you cannot find or do not wish to use a smudge stick, you can buy the ingredients separately and use as a dried mixture. They can be used separately or combined in whatever proportion you find useful or pleasing. This mixture is burned on a charcoal block. The smoke is then blown or fanned into the area. Whatever you do not use can be stored in a tightly covered jar for future use.

Cleansing Your Personal Energy and Aura

Carrying the idea a step further, it is also a good idea to smudge yourself. You do this for all the same reasons you would cleanse a space—when you have been under stress or involved in a confrontational situation, and any time you have been in a position to accumulate a load of unwanted vibrations from within yourself or from the people or environment you have come in contact with. This can be a good way to release the tensions of the day before beginning the evening's activities, and it is especially good to do before engaging in any magical or ritual practice. This will ensure that you do not consciously or unconsciously bring harmful, counterproductive vibrations into another working.

Another simple way of cleansing unwanted negativity and associations from your energy field is to make a spray or mist. Combine about a tablespoon each of **rosemary**, **sage**, **thyme**, and **oregano** in a tea ball and brew a strong tea from them. When it is cooled you can dilute the preparation with as much as a gallon of water. Add a little rubbing alcohol to make sure that the mix does not go bad or grow mold if you plan to keep it on hand for a while. Put it in a spray bottle to mist yourself and your surroundings. It gently removes unwanted energies that are clinging to you and leaves a light, pleasant scent behind.

Cleansing a Negative Environment—Ancient Sacred Incense

Just as weeds accumulate in your garden or dust collects on a neglected shelf, unwanted energies can collect in your living environment. This does not mean that you necessarily live in a harsh or stressful place.

It means that no one is immune from periodic unpleasantness. This could be an accumulation of fatigue and stress from your job or an unhappy relationship. It could be vibrations left over from an illness. It could be the collected energies of disquieting dreams or nightmares.

Another recipe for cleansing and protecting with a spicy and woodsy Oriental aroma is a mixture of equal parts **frankincense**, **myrrh**, and **sandalwood** combined with a few crushed **bay** leaves. These ingredients have been used extensively since ancient times and were highly prized throughout the Old World. This blend works very well when cleansing either a person or a place and also sets a good foundation for deep-level meditation. If you use essential oils in your mixture, you can use it in an infuser. Or if you mix the beads of the resins together, you can burn it on charcoal and use it as a smudge. **Copal** can also be added to this combination and makes both a pleasing and powerful additive. If you wish to give it a lighter touch, you may add a few drops of **neroli**, **bergamot**, or **rose** oil onto the dried mixture. Not only will these elements enhance the scent of the mixture, they also bring about inner lightness and openness to prosperity, love, and all the good things life has to offer. This one works the best when doing a formal cleaning of an area because the smoke interacts with any charges in the air or environment to neutralize negativity and set a natural ward of blessing and protection.

Purging the Space

A third combination of ingredients is Epsom salts (magnesium sulfate or $MgSO_4$), and denatured alcohol. Put about 1/4 cup of Epsom salts in a fireproof dish—preferably a metal one. Then set the dish on a tile, trivet, or flat rock. This combination burns very hot and can scorch the table underneath your container unless it is insulated by the tile. Pour enough denatured alcohol to cover and saturate the Epsom salts, then light the mixture. It burns with a piercing blue flame and, when left in a room to completely burn out, it will purge the vibrations of the space very effectively. This is not a smudge and does not work that well when dealing with the human aura. Nonetheless, it is an excellent addition to the selection of clearing agents as it also has the advantage of not having a thick smoke or pungent odor. Unlike smudge, it will not set off a smoke alarm. This can be a great blessing to those with allergies and other sensitivities to more traditional clearing materials.

Another way to completely clear the energy in a space is to take pure **dragon's blood** resin and put it on a burning charcoal block. It will reduce all vibrations in an atmosphere to absolutely zero. After this is burned away, you can burn the combination of your choice to reset, bless, and seal the space.

Binding a Harmful Influence

Occasionally, you may be aware that another person actively or subconsciously wishes you ill. By this we do not necessarily mean that someone is actually "putting a curse" on you. In truth, curses take time and energy and a certain degree of personal focus, which most people do not possess. In all likelihood, what is happening is that an individual may dislike you or be jealous or resentful of what you do or have, the job you have, what you look like, or who your friends are. This negative and malicious atmosphere can be very uncomfortable even if nothing is ever acted on or verbalized. To compound the situation, it is only human nature to respond to negative treatment with resentment and anger. This forms an attachment—a two-way street of negativity that binds the two participants together with cords of mutual antipathy.

A simple combination of oils that can be used to seal away negative forces and remove this kind of opposition is made from 2 parts each of **ivy** and **orris** for their binding and controlling qualities, and 4 parts **bay** for its powerful protective qualities and its ability to overcome barriers and opposition.

Binding Oil

- 🌿 1 part ivy—binding, honesty
- 🌿 1 part orris—binding, commanding, hex-breaking
- 🌿 2 parts bay—protection, removing barriers and opposition

Occasionally, specific individuals with personal focus and a strong will actively work to disrupt the quality of your personal space and cause you unhappiness and harm. This is called "hexing" and is a term that you will hear used to describe any active form of ill-wishing. Hexing creates blocked or locked up energy patterns and attachments to dead-end situations. It is caused by an active intention on the part of an individual for you to come to harm or misfortune. This is more than a simple run of "bad luck." Let it first be said that this is far more than simply someone wishing you ill. It also requires a two-way connection between you and the individual. It also implies that this is a situation that you have invited or permitted in some way. It requires an equal effort of focus or will and intention on your part to break the bonds of this association. This may require an intense cleansing of your environment and yourself, including cleansing baths and clearing of your space both at home and where you work. It will also require a cycle of meditation and inner work to discover and discontinue the reasons you have allowed this into your life. It will **never** require reverse cursing or any such variant of that idea. To go into that is to create an endless cycle of negativity and harm that will only bind you closer to the individual. It serves no one and solves nothing, as well as violates the principle that no magic or energy work should be done on anyone without their advised consent whatever its cause or reason.

There are also situations in which the nature of a relationship could be described as "psychic vampirism." This is a situation in which an individual seems to sap the strength and energy of the people around him or her. This individual can fasten on a single individual or on a group in general. The effects are not generally seen immediately, but over time a pattern of weakness and debilitation reveals itself attached to circumstances around this individual. It is often seen in personal relationships or in team situations in the workplace. A great deal has been said and written about codependency and destructive cycles, and it should be recognized that in order to free one's self from such a parasitic individual, one must deal with inner issues that cause the continuation of this involvement. This is never a one-way process. Draining energy and sapping your strength is in no way a manifestation of love, nor is enabling and acquiescing to such a situation a manifestation of your devotion. Part of this cycle should include the clearing of one's self and one's environment and, once the clearing is complete, a ritual cycle to encourage inner strength and wholeness to be done as the Moon waxes.

In order for this to effectively release and dispel any of these negative situations, it will be necessary for you to be willing to release the situation and your stake in being right or being vindicated. Whatever your personal agenda for the relationship may have been, it is not going to go that way and you need to release these expectations and the underlying causes for maintaining them. As was previously pointed out, to cling to the idea of getting back at someone is to maintain his or her control over your life and situation. You must also be willing to do what you need to do in the physical world to change the situation. There is no way for you to "win" in this other than by disconnecting yourself and changing your situation. For example, if your supervisor is determined to give you a hard time, you need to either remedy what it is about your person or performance that is causing the disagreement or, failing that, you need to be willing to find another job or request a transfer. Working for peace and happiness in the workplace is not going to be successful if you are not willing to let go of the harmful situation.

Composing an Oil for Binding a Harmful Influence

To make an oil blend for banishing and the binding of problems, choose oils with those specific properties.

For the first step, we will blend an oil composed of scents that banish, cleanse, and protect. The purpose is to dispel the negative circumstances and the inner attitudes that provide them with the fertile ground in which they grow. We are looking for oils that appear in more than one of the categories, if possible. **Rue** appears several times in Appendix A to banish, dispel negativity, and act as a "hex-breaker," that is, it breaks up and disperses blocked or locked up energy that is attached to you. Rue is considered a powerful protective herb in ancient Italian traditions. **Geranium** is also a "hex-breaker" as well as a protector, and will mitigate the sharp scent of the rue. **Cumin** dispels negativity and protects. For power and protection we will add **High John the Conqueror** because it works as a mirror to repel adverse conditions and negative intentions, but only in a very small quantity because these are secondary aspects of the spell and, in a large quantity, would overpower the original intention. This gives us a good selection of scents from which to blend the final oil. Because rue has the principal qualities we are looking for, we will use that as the basis of the oil. To bind the process, add **orris**. Orris also seals the personal energies so that negative influences will be less likely to reattach themselves. So by a process of both selection and elimination here is the recipe for cleansing and purifying the Spirit at the Waning Moon. The result is a cooling and stimulating scent that clears the mind and helps you enter into a state in which you can meditate and use your critical awareness to examine the roots of your difficulty. It also breaks the hold that the negative situation has on your subconscious so that you can view it objectively. This gives you power over the situation rather than the other way around.

Purifying the Spirit Oil

- ⚗ 3 parts **rue**—banishes, dispels negativity, hex-breaker
- ⚗ 3 parts **geranium**—hex-breaker
- ⚗ 3 parts **cumin**—dispels negativity, protects
- ⚗ 2 parts **orris**—binding, sealing
- ⚗ I part **High John the Conqueror**—repels adverse conditions and negativity

If psychic vampirism is the issue, the proportion of cumin can be increased for empowering the individual, and balsam fir or evergreen added to enhance inner clarity and ability to see the situation as it is. These two additives enhance the ability to identify the source of your difficulties and the energy drain it represents. This will go a long way in allowing you to decide on a course of action to restore and safeguard your life energy.

Psychic Protection

There may be other reasons you need psychic protection. Some people are empathic, that is, they sense the feelings of others. While this may be helpful in situations where understanding and cooperation are necessary, it can also be debilitating if the situation involves a high level of negative or other strong emotions. Also, when doing divination or psychic work, it is a good idea to provide yourself with some sort of shielding to make sure that what you are perceiving is only there by your intention and not an overload from a charged atmosphere. Psychic protection gives you a quality of safe inner space while giving you the ability to choose what you wish to perceive.

After purifying and banishing the original situation, this preparation can be used in the ongoing process of working to clear the individual. This process can be made even more potent by using bath salts along with the scented oil as a part of a cleansing and protection ritual. For the base elements choose **frankincense** and **myrrh**. These are

powerful protective and banishing scents that have been used throughout the ages to cleanse, bless, and protect. To specify the intent of the
blend, you may use **amber** or **bergamot**, depending on your prefer-
ence. Each will give the fragrance a distinctive character. Amber has
a warm, sweet, almost musky scent while bergamot has a lighter, citrus smell. Both are also used in work involving love and attraction.
Amber strengthens the basic power of the individual by opening and
reinforcing the heart center. Bergamot increases attraction of material well-being by stimulating clarity and focus. This is the point where
you should carefully consider how the energy drain is most affecting
the energy of the individual, and choose your basic scent accordingly.
Is the impact more material—a drain of money, time, and resources—
or is it emotional and physical—a drain of energy emotion and physical well-being? Adding **yerba santa** increases the power of protection
as it reinforces the dynamic of breaking harmful energy attachments
that have entangled the individual in this draining situation. Its woody,
spicy scent will also balance the sweetness of the main elements. If
you wish, finishing the blend with a hint of **cumin** will complete the
circle by reversing and dispelling any further negativity.

This is only an example of the thought process that goes into blending an oil for your use. There are many essential oils that can be used
for the elements of your blend. Sometimes you will not be able to find
the specific oils that a recipe calls for. At other times there may be
elements in a recipe that you are allergic to or simply that you do not
like. If an oil makes you sneeze outrageously, your eyes water, or
your stomach turn, you will not be able to focus on the rest of the
work and process, regardless of how well-recommended the blend
may be. It is wise to take some time to experiment before making
your final choice. Also, anything you create yourself will always be
more powerful and pertinent than one someone else creates for you,
because your own creations come from your heart and resources.

Psychic Protection Oil

- 2 parts **frankincense**—protection, banishing, blessing
- I part **myrrh**—protection, banishing, blessing
- I part **amber**—strengthens inner power
- I part **yerba santa**—breaks harmful energy attachments
- I part **cumin**—dispels and reverses negativity, protects

Beginning a Transformation—An Inner Journey

The Waning Moon is the time for the first step in the process of transforming your life, both externally in terms of situations and, more importantly, internally in terms of the personal beliefs and inner structures that have created these undesirable circumstances. In Greek mythology, the hero Hercules fought a monster called a Hydra. Its greatest strength lay in the fact that, when one of its heads was cut off, it grew seven more in its place. Only by stabbing it through to the heart was he able to finally kill it. Problems are very much like that. Removing their symptoms will only result in having them crop up again in another form. Only by finding their heart can you be sure that they will no longer trouble you. This is not only the opportunity to simply rid yourself of a problem or negative situation, but an excellent time to work on the roots of a persistent difficulty. The contracting energy of this time provides a good energy matrix for introspective practices such as meditation, self-examination, or past-life regression that will reveal the causes so that you can deal with them directly rather than with their results. Past-life regression and soul retrieval are discussed more fully in the section regarding eclipses, but any time during the darker phases of the Moon is a good time to engage in this type of work.

Removal of a person, situation, or condition from one's life can be a more complex situation than it outwardly seems. We are all familiar with an individual who repeatedly attracts unfortunate relationships. Although the names of the individuals may change, the circumstances duplicate themselves with painful predictability. One hurtful relationship or recurring negative situation is removed only to be replaced by an identical one in short order. The same can be said for failing circumstances—a series of failed jobs or disastrous living situations. When we see this kind of repetitive pattern, it is a good indication that it is not an isolated incident of bad luck or poor planning, but a more deep-seated pattern with roots hidden in the individual's subconscious or past. The roots can be karmic, that is, stemming from incidents in other lifetimes in which the individual made certain decisions. It can be the result of a time of failure and a resulting disaster that now the individual is continually attempting to "get it right" by restaging ancient personal disasters. Of course, this does not work because the individual is not aware of the true nature of the problem, and so it goes on and on—repeating. The Waning Moon provides an energy that is helpful when addressing the roots of the dysfunction so that the problem can be dealt with at its source. It is a good time to do past-life regression work with the intention of soul retrieval and investigation into the causes of negative karmic situations.

When dealing with spells of removal, it is important to deal with the basic cause of your difficulty as well as its present-time results. That is, if you are broke, remove the inner attitudes that result in personal obstacles to having money and abundance. This is often caused by deeper issues of unworthiness and inadequacy. If you have a bad relationship, work with the intention of binding or limiting the effects that person's negative energy is causing and the reasons you attracted the situation in the first place, as well as the reason that you are maintaining the connection. When these reasons are dealt with, removing the person can usually be accomplished far more easily. If your problem is depression or self-inflicted limitations of any sort, work to remove the impact of that limitation. For example, in the case of depression, you would work to bring about optimism and a more positive outlook by revealing the true goodness and worth that is inside you. An important aspect of this process is removing the lies you are telling yourself—morbid reaffirmations of belief in your own lack of ability to succeed in life and to be happy. Removing this delusion of darkness is an important step in moving towards strength and health. Once the immediate problems are set at bay, you can address the deeper roots of the situation—the reasons you have attracted such a situation into your life.

It is considered unethical to work on anyone for any reason without his or her expressed, informed permission. This can present a thorny problem when confronted with the need to remove an obnoxious neighbor or bothersome ex-partner. But there is a real reason behind the prohibition in this case. Simple removal of a person in your life may temporarily remove the cause of the present problem, but it does not remove the underlying reason that you attracted the problem. It is also often the case that these individuals cannot be removed until the reason behind your attachment is resolved. When that is successfully done, you will often see that the negative people or situations will remove themselves without any further effort on your part. It is your attachment to them that causes their presence. Once that attachment is resolved, the negative situation dissolves like mist on a sunny morning.

This is an opportunity to look at the broader issues in the question. It is important to analyze the issue at hand to discover what you really want as an outcome. For instance, when dealing with noisy, obnoxious neighbors, there is a distinct temptation to simply work for their removal. But this does not take into account the likelihood of other ones just like them, or worse, taking their place. Better to look at what you really want. Is it just their removal or do you really want a peaceful, harmonious living arrangement? Working for this is more likely to bring lasting results that are really what you want and it is this time in the Moon's cycle that the energies are strongest to do this type of inner work—very like pulling weeds and planting "root crops."

Preparation—A Ritual Process

If possible, choose a time when you will be by yourself and in private. Fast on juices and clear broth all day, or, if that is not possible, eat lightly, avoiding red meat, caffeine, and sugar. Ideally, you should not be taking any medications other than those specifically prescribed by your healthcare professional. For example, antihistamines and antibiotics can make you sleepy or put you in an otherwise altered state of awareness. If you are ill or medicated, it is a good idea to wait until your health returns before embarking on any magical process. Thoroughly clean the room or space in which you will be doing your work. Wash all working surfaces with salt water. Smudge the area and yourself to purify the vibrations.

Now you can begin the process of looking inward to search for the roots you wish to remove. This may take longer than you think. It may start an ongoing process of self-revelation that clears a great deal more than you first imagined. Or the problem may be revealed with sudden clarity so that this is a short and illuminating process. Whatever the case, be cautioned that the first answer you find is not necessarily the "root" cause, but simply the result or "plant" visible above the surface. Take your time. The Waning Moon is the time for beginning these processes, but this does not imply that this can be accomplished overnight. Be honest with yourself. The roots of any problem lie as much within you as within external forces. It is wise to view these dispassionately without an agenda of self-vindication or blame-giving. Simply allow possibilities to come to you. The more honest and open you are with yourself, the more you will be able to see.

The more you are able to see, the more powerful your results will be. Accept whatever truth you find while setting aside your anger, resentment, fear, or grief. You are not looking for emotion-based explanations, but a true perspective on the situation as it is. A way to begin to analyze and identify the true nature of the problem is by taking careful stock of the effects it is creating in your life. These can be subtle and more far-reaching than what is first visible. Often it is these subtle secondary effects that give you insight on the true nature of the situation.

A good way to begin this is to start a journal dedicated to the issue with which you are dealing. Allow your thoughts to simply flow. Start with the simple ideas and then just discourse about them to your journal. As one thought leads to another, this can often be extremely revealing. Also, writing in a journal forces your mind to objectify the ideas. By using a journal to identify the causes of the problem and the underlying issues and karmic cycles that have played themselves out repeatedly in your life, they cease to be formless feelings that chase each other around your mind, and become a linear construct of events and attitudes that lead one to the other. Once this process is started you will sometimes be led into possibilities and insights that would never have otherwise occurred to you. Once again, give yourself time. Set aside a space of time every night for a week to sit with your journal or your meditations. After purifying yourself, sit with a candle in a quiet space with your journal to allow the ideas to flow into you. Listen to yourself. You are the one who holds the ultimate answers and keys to your situation. This can be a powerful process if you let it develop to its fullest potential.

As a closing gesture, give thanks for the opportunity to learn from these situations and for the lessons you have learned. An attitude of honest gratitude can be more opening and healing than almost any other personal act. Gratitude opens the hands of the Spirit to receive help and enlightenment on many levels. As long as you are resisting a situation, you are holding it away from you. It is only by embracing it and realizing that no matter what the situation or how dark things seem, it is an opportunity to learn and grow that you have brought into your life for a reason. Accepting the situation is accepting yourself. Acceptance with gratitude allows you to release it and move on to more positive circumstances.

As you go about this, or any magical process, it can be very helpful to have a charm or talisman to carry with you. This can be a figure, a pendant, a stone, or any small physical object that reminds you of the work you are doing. You should make it part of your ritual process and have it about you when you do the magical work. You should anoint it with a touch of your oil blend. This will allow it to take on the charge of your intention.

Choosing a Charm

While any small object will do, stones and crystals can make powerful charms because it is the nature of their crystalline structure to take on and resonate with specific vibrations of energy. A well-chosen stone or crystal can bring an added strength to your intention and work. When a crystal is put in line with an electrical charge, it vibrates at a specific frequency that is unique to its type and structure. Putting it in line with your body's electrical field puts you in line with its nature and it will add its specific vibration to your own.

Smoky quartz with **jade** makes a good talisman to calm the mind. In cases where an individual is under stress from his or her environment, this makes a good charm to keep the mind clear. It helps the wearer to sort out which fears are real and which are imagined. It is a good one to wear every day, as this will put the mind in the habit of rational sorting of the environment and eventually lead to greater clarity of thought and discretion.

When an individual has been operating under a certain set of guidelines for a long time, these behavior patterns become fixed and rigid. This can reflect itself in mental and emotional attitudes, and more deeply, in ways of terms of self-image. This leads the individual to self-limiting ways of thinking as well as a limited view of his or her place in the Universe. Thought patterns like this are a serious detriment for any work with personal transformation because they make the individual deny possibilities beyond their limited scope of personal awareness. This leads to a series of inner barriers and self-fulfilling prophecies of failure and limitation. This combination of stones helps alleviate these self-limiting considerations and allows the individual to see him- or herself clearly in respect to the cause of the stress. It also provides the energy needed to step out of these circumstances.

Covellite works to break up these "energy concretions," that is, patterns of energy, thought, and attitudes that have become rigid barriers to change and growth. By breaking up these energy patterns, the individual has the opportunity to move forward and see the roots of these limitations. Covellite helps the user move past blockages and considerations that have been solidified, and allows personal transformation work to continue to move beyond these boundaries. It also reinforces the energy system complex to enable it to form new patterns under the individual's direction. Very often an individual may do a great deal of work to remove blockages and considerations that keep him or her from changing, but before a new life pattern can emerge, the old pattern of the energy fields will reassert itself out of habit. Covellite helps the individual maintain the open matrix of the energy field until the new and more positive pattern of changes takes hold.

A good secondary stone to wear with covellite is **garnet**. Garnet helps strengthen the energy pattern. It provides the individual with an Earth-based energy that can help enable him or her to take full advantage of the new energy patterns that the work will make available.

There are other stones that keep you from attracting problems or harmful influences. One is **malachite**—a bright green stone swirling with darker green that is a carbonate of copper. Malachite is particularly appropriate for issues involving real-world situations such as abundance and prosperity. Stones that act in a similar way are the iron sulfides **marcasite** and **pyrite** that can help you keep the empty spot from filling with outmoded patterns of limitation and attachment once the negative attachments have been released.

The Next Step—The Dark of the Moon

Once you have cleared your inner garden, it is time to move on to the next step of the process. As the Moon grows darker, the energy becomes more introspective until finally it gives no light at all. The Dark of the Moon is the next step in the process, as its powerful contracting influence will allow you to permanently remove the blocks and barriers that are standing in your way.

Chapter 3

Once the cleansing work of the Waning Moon is done, there is a period of three days at the Dark of the Moon, (that is the actual day of the Dark Moon and one day on either side of it) when energies are at their most contracting and its power is at its most introspective. This is an excellent time to rest and reflect on the work you have done. It is a time to do meditation, write in your journal, and allow the process to take hold in your heart and Spirit. It is wisely said that a flower doesn't bloom all the time, and neither should you. The intensity of cleansing should be followed by a time when your vital energies can settle into their new patterns. Get used to having those negative influences gone and prepare for the creative cycle to come. If you are doing serious work of personal transformation, this can be a useful time to take a personal sabbatical. Stay home, sort through your closets, and get rid of things that you no longer want or need on a physical level or on the mental, emotional, and spiritual ones. The effects of cleansing work are not always immediately visible or obvious. A time of quiet is a good idea to allow these changes to take hold before testing them in the energetic spirit of the Waxing Moon to come.

Some traditions have it that no work at all should be attempted at the Dark of the Moon. But if you want something permanently cleared out, this is the most potent time to do that work. More than just clearing space, this is the time for serious removal. Agricultural lore tells us that the Dark of the Moon is the time to pull up stumps so they will not sprout again, and so it is with the situations in your life.

This is a time of purging and preparation for renewal. If there is any seriously unwanted energy in your life, this is the time to work on its removal so that, when the Moon begins its increase, you can begin reconstruction, knowing that you have a clear field to work on and that leftovers of old business will not return to mar the new work. If you need to make a permanent severance, this is the time. This is the moment to break with the past.

Fasting and Clearing

The idea of fasting or abstaining from food and drinks is found across all cultures and traditions. Christian Lent and Muslin Ramadan are two well-known examples of the idea of denying the body to strengthen the Spirit. In the ancient Hindu healing tradition of Ayurvedic medicine, it is recommended that an individual abstain from solid food at least one day a week to allow the digestive system to clear. To many people, the concept of fasting conjures up images of rag-thin holy men and personal deprivation. In extreme circumstances this may be so, but there are many lesser degrees of fasting that can be physically beneficial and spiritually cleansing. The Dark of the Moon is a good time to take a day to allow the physical system to rest while you prepare yourself spiritually to release unwanted circumstances and energies.

Choose a day when you will be able to spend your time quietly in peace and privacy. This does not mean taking a Saturday to rush all over town running errands by yourself. It means choosing a day to spend resting and in contemplation, perhaps doing low-impact activities that you enjoy, such as spending time in your garden or doing artistic crafts. Perhaps it means going to the park or the seashore to enjoy the beauties of nature. Because this phase of the Moon lasts three days (one day on each side of the actual aspect), it is highly possible to schedule a convenient time for this.

Fasting of this type does not mean starving yourself painfully. Ideally, you should refrain from solid food and red-blooded meats, such as beef or chicken. Also, you should refrain from non-clear beverages, such as milk, and those that contain caffeine or alcohol. Instead, drink fruit and vegetable juices that have been freshly prepared. If you are able, it is best to prepare the juice yourself the night before. If you cannot make your own juice, a health-food store will have a variety of natural juices that have a full spectrum of nutrients as opposed to commercial preparations whose processing and packaging (such as metal cans) seriously depletes or destroys much of the nutritional value. For a day as you rest and meditate, drink only these natural juices, water, and herbal (non-caffeinated) tea. There are also tea blends available that are made especially for this time.

A word of caution: If you have a specific medical condition such as diabetes or hypoglycemia that might be adversely affected even for a day, consult your healthcare professional first before doing this. He or she can best advise you and may be able to suggest an alternative regimen that will be safe and effective for you.

This gentle practice can be a valuable assistance in allowing both body and spirit to clarify their energies. It will also provide you with a specifically designated time for meditation in which to enhance your magical process.

Intuition and Divination

There are some traditions that tell us that the Dark of the Moon is a good time for divination. The reasoning behind this is that while the Moon's light increases its energy, it also focuses its energy on the processes needed for growth and relating to the physical world. Its energy becomes extroverted. The intensely introspective energy of the Dark of the Moon provides a time when the intuitive awareness will not be distracted and the clearest inner vision is possible.

The word *intuition* literally means "taught from within," meaning our ability to listen to that inner voice that tells us what our physical senses do not. It is the ability to focus subconscious impressions of external events of which we are not consciously aware and translate them through the lens of higher awareness into conscious, purposeful actions. These subliminal impressions can be physical in nature—the angle of light, a gesture seen out of the corner of your eye, a line of a newspaper that has been glimpsed, a barely audible sound—all are perceived, but not strongly enough to register as a conscious image or impression. Animals in the wild have these sensitivities as they react to the almost imperceptible stimuli of wind, temperature, pressure, and scent. What does a flock of birds sense that causes them to suddenly take flight when they are being watched by a predator? These wild creatures are apparently attuned to their environment on more than the physical level. Their senses have been refined by ages of evolution to sense the movement of forces on many levels. It has been demonstrated that some animals have an awareness of electromagnetic fields. Others sense subtle changes in ocean currents or intensity and duration of light. There are ranges of perceptions beyond the physical five that we as humans acknowledge that allow these creatures to sense currents in their world and react immediately, which gives them an edge for survival. It is, therefore, not impossible to assume that human beings have a vestigial capacity for such an awareness, although our evolution has left conscious perception of it far behind. These are all impressions that bypass the rational, cognizant mechanisms of our thinking brain and imprint on our subconscious selves. It is called *sub*conscious because it operates behind the scenes as we live our daily lives.

Every one of us, indeed, every living organism is receiving such messages all the time. We can see this in operation in the sensitivity that pets have to the moods of their owners and the heightened awareness that mothers have to their babies' needs. Intuition is a natural ability inherent in all creatures. Our remote ancestors were much closer to these animal tribes, both in terms of evolutionary development and because they relied on them for food and other raw materials. Like animals, our ancestors had access to their subtle senses. They reacted to these stimuli as a part of their survival mechanisms. Like our ancestors, we have these abilities today, passed down in our primal heritage as part of our necessary skills for survival. Sometimes these subconscious signals come from being aware of the small details of the surrounding physical world. They are a compilation of many tiny details that are too small for the conscious mind to notice and so are processed into subtle signals by the unconscious mind. When these promptings become strong enough, we call them "hunches" or "gut-level feelings." But there is more to intuition than physical details.

We can take this a step further. Every being, every element of Creation, is part of the Greater Universe. On the physical plane, this Universe manifests as energy. This energy shows itself in the form of atoms that make up the elements that are the building blocks of all physical creation. In subtler form, this energy manifests as light and sound. And on a more subtle level still, it manifests in the cycles and patterns that govern the interaction of all denser forms of physical creation. Energy moves in currents and flows like weather patterns. This Universe that we physically see and participate in is the reflection of a complex pattern of energies that are in constantly changing motion. We are part of this Universe of flowing energy. This is the stuff of which we are made, just like everything that surrounds us. It is not as great a step as you may think to reach with the heart and mind and be aware of these currents and patterns.

There is also the question of how to cultivate this ability in individuals whose latent gifts may not be as strong: a way to shore up these tenuous gifts and gain reliable access to this special and valuable source of information. It needs to be grounded, at least in part, in a physical system so that its signs can be read and interpreted consistently. Humans, who have developed a tool for every other practice they wish to control and amplify, have developed tools for this purpose as well. The practice of *divination* arose as a tool for the development and clarification of *intuition*, a concrete way to take subconscious impressions and turn them into cognizant communication.

Over the centuries, virtually every civilization we know of has developed its own particular system of divination. The specific details are as widely varied as the peoples who have developed them. The important fact about any system is that it triggers a subconscious reaction in the practitioner to open his or her awareness to the unseen world where the patterns and forces that influence and dictate events on this plane are visible. They are the way we "give ourselves permission" to attune to the inner voices. The divinatory system forms a bridge that connects the reader with the faculty to sense what is and what is about to be—the intuition—while giving that individual a concrete set of images with which to translate those impressions into useful information. These images can be the pictures on a deck of cards, the pattern of tea leaves in a cup, the way a group of coins fall—the list is long.

No matter what method or set of symbols is used, the most important element of any system is its ability to trigger the intuition of the individual. Any divination system is a means of communication between the unseen world and this one. Divination demonstrates our participation and interaction with the energies and forces that move us. By it we become consciously sensitized to these energies, we learn to recognize the feeling of their pressures and currents.

Objective Divination—Physical Systems of Symbols

Divination can be broken down into two basic types. The first we will call *objective* systems. These are the methods that involve an external set of symbols such as tarot card or runes. They work on the idea that certain forms, images, or symbols have a close connection to the currents of energy that manifest themselves as the circumstances or events in our lives. When subjecting these objects to random motion, such as shuffling or tossing, we allow these energies to affect their order and placement. By observing this order, we can objectively decipher which forces are strongest at the moment in a given situation and how they will move in the time to come.

As we engage in this process, it is important to be able to open ourselves to the messages they are presenting to us. We need to be able to open ourselves to intuitive interpretation of the combination of the individual symbols.

Subjective Divination—Dowsing, Pendulums, and Scrying

We will call the second basic type of divination *subjective*. This involves setting the conscious mind one step back to allow the inner hidden self to express itself. This involves the practice of using pendulums or rods, which is generally known as dowsing. These methods use a physical object such as a hanging pendant for a pendulum or loosely held pair of rods or forked stick for dowsing that allows the subconscious mind to relay its message through minute muscular tensions of the hands and physical body. These systems require not only a certain level of inner relaxation, but the ability on the part of the reader to set aside any personal agenda of outcome-based desire in order not to unconsciously prejudice and direct the motion of the tools. They are intended to allow the reader to enter a mild level of altered awareness so that the subtle subconscious reactions can surface while the reader is still in a sufficiently conscious state to intellectually understand and decipher the images or impressions being received. This is commonly known as scrying.

Crystal gazing and gazing into a pool of black ink in a shiny bowl or into a black mirror are forms of scrying. The idea is to fixate and soften the focus of the physical senses so that the inner senses can see more clearly. This is an extremely subjective method with no clear-cut physical path to follow. Therefore, it requires a degree of relaxation and an ability to allow the rational mind to step aside so that these inner impressions can come to the surface.

Making a Black Mirror

The Dark of the Moon is a good time to make your personal scrying mirror. A black mirror, like a crystal ball, allows you to set aside your rational daily thinking process and step aside to become aware of the quiet inner voices and visions that are linked to the Greater Universe. It allows you to see things that are manifesting on the energy plane even though you may not be personally connected to them in your conscious waking state. You may see past events, present-time happenings, or what may lie in the future. Its purpose is to absorb the mundane light and allow a Spiritual Light to be seen within its depths. It does this by giving your conscious mind a point of focus that contains no visual world stimulus. Making the mirror should be a ritual process. After all, this is a tool that you will use in your magic, and it is important to do this in a prepared, cleansed space. This is a process of attunement to the materials and their eventual product.

A black mirror can be made with a piece of glass, black latex paint, a brush, and something to act as a border. You will also need a very fine grit sandpaper to scuff the back side of the glass so the paint will adhere to it. Any piece of glass will do, concave chemical dishes also make an excellent choice, as the curving sides reflect into the bowl. Scrying mirrors can be of any size you like from a small 3″ × 5″ up to full length. Decide which side you will use to "see" with and which you will make the back. Place the glass face down, and scuff the back thoroughly until the entire surface looks slightly cloudy. Wipe the surface clean of any dust and paint it with a coat of the black paint. When this first coat is dry, put on another coat of paint. Do each coat in an attitude of meditation, holding your purpose firmly in mind. As you apply the paint, envision your mirror becoming charged with your intention to be a window to see what is true and what you need to know. Do the same once more for three coats total, charging the mirror as you apply each coat. Let the entire piece dry for at least 24 hours to be sure the paint has completely cured. When the paint is thoroughly dry, put a piece of felt, paper, or cardboard over the back to protect it from scratches. You can also put some of your attunement and scrying oil formula onto the backing to give it a final energy attunement.

Once the entire piece is complete, you are ready to charge it to your purpose. This will "seal" the charge you put into it while painting it and make it ready for your personal use. Remember, this is your personal tool and should be kept for your use alone. If someone else wants to try this, you can make one for them or they can make their own.

After cleansing the space, use the Opening and Scrying scent described here to charge and open the space. Use the oil to make incense that will fill the space with visionary scent. Going a step further, bath salts made with this oil can greatly enhance the visionary experience. Light two indigo, purple, or white candles and place them on either side of the mirror so that it will reflect their flames. Hold the mirror in both your hands or place it on a stand where your eyes will rest on it naturally without effort. Relax into a meditative state and allow your eyes to diffuse your vision. As you do this, you may see the mirror begin to "fill with smoke" or it might become cloudy or seem to ripple. When this happens, you will begin to see symbols or events flash across the dark surface. Be open to them and what they might mean to you personally. Let yourself observe the scenes or symbols that reveal themselves and recognize any emotions that may be connected to them. Later, when the session is completed, you can write down what you saw and analyze what meaning it may have for you. When you are done, cleanse the area and mirror of extraneous vibrations and ground and center yourself. Wrap the mirror carefully or put it in a bag you have made for this purpose and put it away carefully.

Composing an Oil for Developing Intuition and Divination

A ritual attunement process can provide a good bridge by which you relax and allow yourself to attune to your inner awareness. Blends that enhance this type of work are formulated for awareness and attunement. Essences that pertain to intuitive development of any kind come in two types: ones that increase awareness and attunement, and others that encourage relaxation and openness. Those in the latter category tend to be mildly euphoric and encourage an enhanced state of awareness. Before using any essences, it is important to be advised of their properties because they affect different people to differing degrees.

A word of caution: You should never use such a preparation if you are intending to operate machinery or a moving vehicle. Just because a blend is herb-based and natural does not make it any less powerful to your mind and body. Such essences include mugwort, wormwood, galangel, poppy, and cinquefoil.

That being said, any blend you make for this purpose should include elements of both types of essences. It is not useful to completely bliss out and be unable to communicate or interpret your impressions. It is also not useful if you heighten your state of awareness to the point that you cannot relax and open to your inner voices.

Begin with an oil that attunes to higher vibrations, such as **redwood**, for your base. Then add an essence that increases spirituality as well as protection; **sandalwood** is a good choice. Then add an essence that increases openness and relaxation, such as **mugwort**. This combination forms the core of your blend. Finally, add some **ylang-ylang** to the mix. This will lighten the scent as well as bring its distinctive character of protection, balance, and relaxation without being excessively centering or grounding. The result is a heady, woody mixture with light overtones that can encourage inner openness and clarity.

Divination Blend 1–Awareness and Attunement Oil

- 5 parts **mugwort**—openness, relaxation
- 2 parts **redwood**—higher vibrations
- I part **sandalwood**—spirituality, protection
- I part **ylang-ylang**—balance, protection, relaxation

If you prefer a sweeter, more flowery blend, begin with a **light sandalwood** or **galangel**. Enhance it with **poppy** to open your consciousness. And finish it with **ylang-ylang** and a dash of **bergamot** that will lift it with a slight citrus brightness of consciousness as well as adding the benefit of psychic protection. Each blend has its benefits and advantages. It might be wise to experiment with combinations to find a good balance.

Divination Blend 2–Opening and Scrying Oil

- 4 parts **bergamot**—psychic protection, strength
- 2 parts **poppy**—clairvoyance, divination, dreams, balance
- I part **galangel**—psychic powers, protection
- I part **ylang-ylang**—balance, protection, relaxation

Choosing a Charm for Intuition and Divination

Seraphenite (gem clinochlor) is a chatoyant green and silver stone that is helpful in divination because it enables the user to let go of control issues. Often a major block to divination and scrying is the firm hold you have over your own version of reality. Scrying and divination are both processes in which it is necessary to let go of the boundaries of our reality and observe the currents of others that might be. For some, this is not easy. Seraphenite helps the individual release that grasp to allow impressions to come more freely.

Lapis lazuli is an ancient charm for divination and psychic awareness of all kinds. Because of the pyrite stars that twinkle in its rich midnight blue matrix, it was said to connect the wearer to the celestial realms. It is a powerful charm for opening the third eye and all psychic and divinatory talents.

Grounding and Centering—
Coming Back to Earth

Once you have completed your psychic work, it is time to bring yourself down to the present here-and-now by reconnecting to the strong Earth-based energies. We call this *grounding* and *centering*. It is a process by which you allow the heightened energies of metaphysical work and magical practice to return to the universal pool of energies and redirect your own energies to a more balanced flow, connecting to both Earth and heavens.

Everyone has a natural balance and harmony of energy levels that they maintain. This changes from time to time, depending on your relative health and state of mind. When you work with higher-level energies, there will be times that the energies you are dealing with get "a little too much," when you retain more of their intensity and/or content than you wish to, or when you are connected to other levels of consciousness that take you away from your present-time awareness. This can happen easily when you have found it necessary to draw on an extra amount of energy to accomplish a specific purpose such as a healing or divination. When you have accomplished your purpose and the task is accomplished, it is time to reestablish your regular, natural energy level and inner balance. Sometimes you can just get overwhelmed by being in an extremely energetic environment, and after you leave you would like to return to your own natural levels. What you need to do is "ground out."

Grounding literally means to let the excess energy flow back into the base from which it came. There is a pool of Universal Energy that exists all the time. It is from this endless source that you draw your own energies and any extra that you need to accomplish a task. So when you are done with it, you can just let it flow back.

Grounding Exercise

Take a quiet moment to take a deep breath. As you exhale, imagine that the excess energy is flowing downward through your feet and into the ground—all the way into the center of the glowing heart of the Earth. It is important to flow the excess energy all the way down because you do not wish to have it just soaking into the carpet or hanging around in your basement. It should go all the way back to its source. If you prefer, imagine a pure white star as the source of all Universal Energy. As you exhale, send the excess energy as a beam of light back to the star to be purified and reabsorbed. Either way you choose, be sure you send the energy all the way back. Then, take another deep breath and feel your energy come back into balance. Connect to the center of the Earth through your feet and the star above you in the heavens. Find your center between them with another deep breath.

Composing a Grounding Oil

An oil blend can be helpful when you want to ground and reestablish your center quickly. A quick breath from the appropriate formula can help bring you back to Earth gently and restore the harmony of your basic energy levels. Choose a combination of fragrances that are both earthy and warm, and light and refreshing so that you will feel comfortable in your body as well as regain your mental clarity and focus. **Patchouli** is an earthy scent that works well with grounding as well as having the added benefit of being psychically protective. This will help you release any lingering attachments that you may have to the altered state of divination and other-plane energies. The fresh citrus scents of **lemongrass** and **orange** will relax you as well as clear the cobwebs away.

Grounding and Centering Oil

- 5 parts **patchouli**—grounding, psychic protection
- 7 parts **lemongrass**—refreshing, uplifting
- 2 parts **sweet orange**—relaxing, clearing

Radical Severance

Just as the Full Moon is a fine time for handfastings and weddings because it encourages permanence and lasting bonds, so the Dark of the Moon is the time for endings and partings that you want to last. The farmers say that if you want to pull out noxious deep-rooted vines and tree roots so that they do not resprout and return, the Dark of the Moon is the very best time. So it is with relationships. When a situation cannot be resolved, and after all the details of the situation have been put to rest, there is a need to make a final and formal dissolution of the bonds that held the situation together. Make sure that all the details are taken care of—the household goods divided, the legal issues finalized, the locker or desk at work cleared out so that nothing can return to haunt you once this process is done. In the case of divorce or separation, when there are issues that will continue to bind the couple such as children or business issues, make sure the legal issues are as clearly defined as possible. This process is intended to allow the emotional and spiritual bonds to be dissolved so that all participants can continue with their lives in the most free and positive manner, leaving old entanglements behind.

Cutting the Cord and Burning the Broom

A simple ritual involves a piece of light cord, two black candles, two fireproof bowls, a knife or scissors, and a picture of the couple (if it is a work situation, a symbol of the individual involved with the group or company should be found). If no combined image is available, a pair of simple poppets can be made to represent the parties involved. Be sure you make the poppets out of something light that burns easily. Muslin lightly stuffed with tissue will work just fine. A tightly stuffed poppet will be difficult for the flame to consume completely unless you are throwing it into a bonfire. (For more information on making a poppet, see pages 150-151.) Failing that, you may even draw stick figures with crayon on a piece of paper, labeling each one of them. Make sure that if it is a photograph or drawing, it is an image in which the two parties involved can be easily separated. All parties involved do not have to be present or even informed. This is simply a process intended to cut the cords that bind you to whatever situation that needs to be released. This is not work on another person, it is about your inner process to free you from the past and allow a more positive future to take shape unencumbered. You can do this alone or with a group of people who will help you. Remember, this is your magic to act in your life.

Light the two candles while making an appropriate declaration, stating that at this time it is your intention to sever all bonds between the parties, leaving each free on all levels—mental, emotional, physical, and spiritual—to go their separate ways with harm to none. This is very important. This is not a process in which harm should come to anyone involved. Anger and resentment form as firm a bond between parties as love and respect. This is a process to release the energy so that the participants are free of all attachments. You must be willing to release your anger, pain, agendas, and issues following a period of meditation and clearing of yourself. Bind the picture or symbols with a tangle of string or light cord so that all elements are held together. In the case of a photograph, wrap the string around it several times and tie it in the center. If this is a case of separation of a handfasting, the ideal cord to use would be the one that joined the participants' hands at the ceremony (if this was done, and if it is available). If the handfasting cord is not available, then any cord will do.

Anoint yourself or the parties involved with the severance oil (pages 59-60). Then, anoint the image with it, making sure all parties involved are touched with it. Pour your intention into the image so it is firmly fixed in your mind and heart that this is an image of those people bound together. Once this idea is clearly fixed in your mind, take the knife or scissors and cut the cords that bind them, seeing in your mind all energy bonds between them being released and vanishing. Next, cut the picture in half so that the parties are separated. Take each image separately, along with half of the binding cord, and set it alight in the flame of a candle—one for each. Then drop each flaming image into a separate bowl. Let them burn out completely to ash while seeing in your mind that the smoke of the fire carries away any attachments they might have. Each is now separate—whole and complete within themselves without bond on either side.

A word of caution: Make sure that you are doing this in a well-ventilated area away from other flammable material, such as draperies. A fireplace is a good place to do this because it is a fire-safe area and the chimney will carry any smoke up and away. If you do not have a fireplace, have two fireproof bowls (metal or ceramic) on hand that have been placed on fireproof trivets. Open the windows so that any smoke will be quickly dispersed. Never leave any burning material unattended. This process is not intended to result in a large leaping blaze, but it is wiser to err on the side of caution and make sure that you have taken all possible precautions ahead of time.

If this is a separation after a handfasting, this is also the time for you to burn the handfasting broom you jumped. If you are going to burn your broom, it is best to burn it either outdoors on a bonfire built specifically for the occasion, or, if this is not an option, in a fireplace. Even a small broom makes too much smoke to be adequately burned in a bowl. When you do burn it, anoint both shaft and brush with the severance oil. If the timing does not permit the broom to be burned at the same time the rest of the ritual is done, you may incorporate it into the ritual, anointing it and making whatever declaration of separation you feel is appropriate, then sealing it in a plastic bag until you can go somewhere to burn it.

A larger version of this process should also include burning incense and taking a bath with bath salts made from this formula. The more complete your ritual, the more complete your state of mind and heart will be, and the better it will work in your life.

Composing a Severance Oil

Rue is an ideal choice of essence for this purpose. Its nature cuts both ways, making sure that the attachments are removed on all sides. Adding **dragon's blood** to the mixture will give it power as well as protection. Then, consider that this must also include clarity and healing so that life can begin again, refreshed and renewed. For this, choose an herb of the Sun, such as **bay**. It is specifically indicated for endings, exorcism, release, transformation, as well as overcoming opposition, breaking energy bonds on all levels, and bringing balance, harmony, wisdom, and purification. It is also a powerful healer of the heart.

Peppermint, ruled by Mercury, brings similar qualities as well as being uplifting, antidepressant, and renewing. Make a scent bag or other vehicle so that you can carry the fragrance with you for one full cycle of the Moon. At night, before going to sleep, anoint your pressure points—especially your temples, wrists, heart, and the back of your neck—and meditate not only on the severing of the bonds, but on your own return to joy and freedom. Use this cycle of meditation to construct the image of your new life, which is free from the crippling negative entanglements of the old situation. See yourself new and reborn. When the cycle is done, dispose of the bag any way you wish.

Severance Oil

- 2 parts **peppermint**—renewal, transformation, happiness
- 2 parts **dragon's blood**—banishing, power, protection
- 1 part **rue**—banishing, dispels negativity, healing
- 5 parts **bay**—endings, release, transformation, healing

Chapter 4

While the Moon was waning, the work of clearing and removing was taking place. During its full Dark, the major work of clearing obstacles was accomplished, and now, as she begins to grow towards Full, it is time to take advantage of the space you cleared to improve your life and circumstances. Weeds and old growth that choked the space and shaded the Earth from the Sun's light, sapping the strength and drawing energy away from new sprouts have been removed to free the Earth for more positive pursuits. This is the "Spring" of the month. As the Moon grows, its energy becomes more expansive and nurturing. In gardening, this is the time to plant your seeds and take cuttings to root and grow new plants. In magic, it is time to plant the seeds for situations and circumstances that we want to see come about in a short period of time. The Moon's creative energy is not yet at its full strength, and so the magic that you do at this time deals with short-term projects intended to bloom quickly. It is not yet time to change your life, but it is time to work for changing your immediate circumstances. This is a time to prime the pump of *beginnings*. Lifting your spirits can pave the way for larger work done later on. Oils and their derivatives such as bath salts and incense that you make at this time will carry this energy of lightness and new beginnings to be saved for any time of the month when you feel you need a quick pick-me-up.

Mental Clarity

The first step in this process is dispelling the fog of introspection that was so useful during the darker phases. This is the time to begin looking outward rather than inward and to extend your power and energy into the material world to create the circumstances you would like to see come into your life. At this time, it's a good idea to blend a formula that you can take with you in a small vial to sniff when you feel the need to clear your mind and heart, and also to use for a wider range of products, such as bath salts, if you feel the need for a more extensive mental house-cleaning. To bring about a change of mind and heart, light a yellow or orange candle. Yellow is the color of Mercury that rules mental processes. Orange is the color associated with the Sun that will dispel all shadows and darkness. Step into a warm bath with the Sun-bringer oil mixed into bath salts, and allow your spirits to lift and clear as the water soaks away the blockages and stiffness in your physical and energy bodies.

Clary sage clears the mind and memory, opening the way for the learning process. It is also known for its powerful ability to alleviate symptoms of PMS and seasonal sun-deprivation disorders. Mix this with **lavender** to balance, center, and stimulate.

Members of the **citrus** family are very potent in dispelling all sorts of mental fog. Because of their high volatility, they are not long-lasting, but the brightness and clarity of focus they bring can be a joyful relief. If you are spending long hours at the computer or studying, a quick breath of tangerine or **grapefruit** can restore mental acuity and reduce fatigue in short order. **Tangerine** is a specific for creativity and inspiration. They are also strongly antidepressant and will give a quick lift of spirits. **Bitter orange** specifically addresses the mind and spirits, as opposed to **sweet orange** whose powers address the heart and emotions.

Heliotrope is often called the Sun-bringer because of its power to drive away the darkness. It banishes the fog while calming the Spirit and opening the heart to optimism, allowing the work of the other oils to do their work more effectively. Heliotrope is also less volatile than the citruses and will reinforce their effect and make them last much longer.

Sun-Bringer Oil

In this order, blend:

- 🌿 4 parts **lime**—antidepressant, stimulant, strength
- 🌿 2 parts **clary sage**—harmony, balance, memory, concentration
- 🌿 2 parts **lavender**—centering, harmony, balance, strength, stimulant
- 🌿 3 parts **bitter orange**—happiness, stimulant, relaxing
- 🌿 I part **heliotrope**—optimism, calming

Personal Empowerment

It is also important during this time to assert certain personal changes that you may want to see in your life. It is not yet time to work fundamental changes in your basic core structure, but enhancing your charisma and confidence might not be a bad thing. For personal empowerment, **bay** is a rich-smelling oil that puts a great deal of fast-acting power into wherever it is added. It will encourage inner and outer harmony and balance while overcoming opposition, whether this comes from within you or from outside. Bay also has transformative properties and will help you initialize the changes you want to make while attracting the energies you are looking for. In Northern California, bay grows alongside the giant Redwood trees. Their combined smell is almost euphoric in nature. **Redwood** also encourages harmony and balance while connecting you to higher-plane energies and opening you to wisdom. Adding **amber** to this combination adds the sweetness of attraction as well as strength of spirit. To complete this process, light a red or rose-colored candle. Write your wish or intention for this empowerment on a bay leaf, and then burn it on a charcoal block or with the candle flame. As it reduces to ash, and its fragrance fills the air, feel the empowerment fill you.

Personal Empowerment Oil

- 🌿 3 parts **bay**—protection, release, transformation, attraction
- 🌿 3 parts **redwood**—empowerment, wisdom, connection to Higher Energies
- 🌿 2 parts **amber**—protection, strength, attraction, happiness

Choosing a Charm for Personal Empowerment

Yellow stones correspond to the energy of Mercury; therefore, they are connected with all kinds of mental clarity and agility. Using a yellow stone as a charm can allow you to focus more easily while the bright energy of the stone drives out the cobwebs and encourages optimism.

Yellow topaz is particularly powerful for encouraging optimism. It resonates with a vibrant harmonic of joy and cleverness that can cheer you on the darkest day. It is also highly effective in helping you to clarifying your thought processes while making plans.

Heliodore is a form of beryl, the stone family that emerald comes from. Heliodore acts in a more emotional way than topaz. It promotes cleverness and a sense of inner joy combined with pride in one's own accomplishments. Its nature is creative and individualistic, and this encourages laughter and artistic creativity. It is particularly effective in treating grief and loss by opening the wearer to the possibilities of life in the future by helping the Spirit to find its own bright nature and joy in life. Its color is caused by uranium oxide, which encourages a slight distancing from the physical level of the body, allowing the wearer to release grosser or blocked energies that have interlocked with the physical body vibration.

Amber is petrified tree resin. It is extremely powerful in discharging and rebalancing the body's electrostatic field, which makes it very helpful in treating shock from raising intense levels of energy, whether these increased energies have come from hard work or intense emotion. It has a brightening and calming nature that encourages self-esteem. Amber is soft enough to carve easily and has been made into a wide variety of charms throughout the ages. If you choose amber for your talisman, it is a good idea to use a shape that corresponds to your purpose. A Sun-shape or goddess figure might be a good idea, because this also carries the thought-form energy of fertility, creativity, and brightness of Spirit.

Orange stones correspond to the Sun's courageous energy of self-assurance and vitality. They are a wise choice when you are working for increased confidence and self-esteem along with courage and renewal of the heart.

Citrine is an orange variety of the quartz family. It will light the heart and help the wearer find courage and optimism. It will help you find the light inside you to make your way through troubled times, and courage and confidence to face new situations. If a child is having nightmares and is afraid of the dark, a citrine hung around his or her neck or hung by the bed can help him or her find peaceful sleep and courage to face these fears.

Carnelian comes in a range of colors from pale orange to deep red. It helps the wearer to dispel all forms of negativity, whether this comes from external sources or is self-generated. It strengthens the inner sense of identity and well-being through self-esteem so that negativity cannot find a place to take hold and will be easier to dispense with if it does. Wear a carnelian to a job interview for more confidence and inner strength. Carnelian will help you stand your ground in a confrontational situation, and through this sense of inner strength, to get your point across without panicking or becoming overly emotional. There is a folk belief in China that carnelian will ward off demons and can be carried for good luck and protection. Like amber, carnelian is often found carved into charms. Find one that is appropriate to your purpose.

Lucky Mojo

While transforming your whole life may take some time, giving yourself a break can definitely be a good thing. Waxing Moon Luck Magic may not reverse an entire downward spiral cycle, but it can give a momentary bounce to fortunes and, by association, lift your spirits considerably. It is certainly a commentary on the human condition in general to see that there are as many herbs and oils attributed to luck as there are to protection and love, and there are many more of them than those dedicated to higher spiritual awareness.

When choosing oils for a fast-luck blend, you need to think about what sort of luck you want to attract. Oils that you would choose for a "Have a Good Day" spell would be different than one you would blend to give you the edge if you were going to a casino for the night. A blend of this kind will be fast-acting, but will not last more than a day or evening—but such is the fickle nature of Lady Luck. This is a blend that you would use to rub on your pocketbook or wallet and onto the palms of your hands. **Cinquefoil (five finger)** and **mandrake** are both old-fashioned traditional luck-bringers. Adding cinquefoil to any spell is said to tip the odds in your favor and increase the power of your magic and magnetism to all good things. Mandrake draws all forms of material power and prosperity. For this kind of fast-working formula, you need to add something that binds firmly and quickly, and so we add **sweet pea** because of the plant's tendency to twine and bind wherever it grows. **Bindweed (wild morning glory)** tends to choke out other plants, and **traditional morning glory** can be fickle and release before you achieve your desired results. The aroma of sweet pea will also soften the musky odor of the mandrake and make it more pleasant to wear and use. If you cannot find mandrake oil or do not like the smell, you may substitute mistletoe, which has similar properties.

Fast-Luck Oil

- 1 part **cinquefoil (five finger)**—good luck
- 1 part **mandrake** or **mistletoe**—material gain, power, prosperity
- 2 parts **sweet pea**—binds

Choosing a Charm for Lucky Mojo

While a rabbit's foot and four-leaf clover are traditional charms, luck charms come in a wide variety of shapes and sizes. Some people have a lucky scarf or necklace. Others have a small object they keep in their pocket. Some people carry them all the time and would not go out without them. Others only carry them when they need to feel lucky. It should be said here that half the secret to "luck" is your attitude. If you go out expecting the worst, certainly the worst will find its way to you. But if you put your attention on optimistic possibilities and look for good things to happen, this definitely opens the door for good things to come your way. By using a stone or crystal, you can tap into the stone's energetic nature that will make your own energy field more receptive to the kind of results you're looking for. While there are just as many choices for lucky stones as there are other kinds of charms, green stones are connected with fertility and creativity as well as health and regeneration. Anoint the stone with the oil blend while focusing on the type of luck you desire.

Green tourmaline's nature allows it to automatically engage with your personal energies. Its green color will engage with your heart energy to surround you with a strong field that encourages growth, expansion, and good possibilities.

Moss agate looks like moss or ferns under water. These plant-like structures are caused by inclusions of hornblende in the quartzite matrix of the stone. Hornblende energizes the mental faculties, while the quartz surrounding it connects its energy with all the energy systems of your body. Focus on the green and growing appearance of the plant-like structures in the stone and feel the energy of the stone work on the energies surrounding you to draw good circumstances and opportunities.

Short-Term Abundance

There are times when our budgets need a quick boost. At such times, burn a green candle with your wish for the amount of money written into the wax. Anoint the candle with a fast-cash oil to bring in the emergency funds that you need. This is slightly different from fast luck in that it is specifically targeted to your finances. But remember, that no matter what kind of magic you are doing, the last step is always to move toward your goal in the physical world. All the luck and prosperity magic in the world will not bring you riches if you sit at home just moping and hoping. It requires action on your part to make the way for this abundance to come to you.

To blend such an oil, choose a prosperity fragrance that specifies money, such as **clove**, as your base fragrance. Clove is particularly fast-acting and also carries overtones of protection and well-being. **Allspice** can be added to the clove because its two principal virtues are strength of will and prosperity/money. When **bayberry** is added, it deepens the scope of the prosperity to include well-being and domestic happiness, as well as wealth and material gain. Then choose an oil to put power behind the wish. A good choice for this is **spikenard** because its primary function is commanding and power, which focuses power from deep within you and will connect you strongly with your desire. The combination will not only be a fast-acting prosperity oil, but will smell like delicious Christmas cookies baking.

Fast-Money Oil

- 8 parts **bayberry**—prosperity, good luck, material prosperity and well-being, wealth, domestic happiness, house blessing
- 3 parts **clove** (quick acting)—prosperity, money, well-being
- 1 part **allspice**—strength of will, material gain
- 4 parts **spikenard**—commanding

Choosing a Charm for Short-Term Abundance

For abundance magic, it is a good idea to choose a stone that is strongly connected to earthy energies, because it is the physical plane you are seeking to manipulate. In work of this type, you are not necessarily looking for spiritual well-being, but well-being of your physical life circumstances. Both malachite and Tiger's-eye have long been connected to this kind of work. Be advised that malachite is soft and will get chipped and scratched if you carry it in your pocket, but Tiger's-eye is very hard and makes a durable talisman. Both stones are often found carved into charms that will also suit the mental process of your work. Frog and fish, as well as elephant, shapes are often associated with abundance and prosperity.

Malachite is made from oxides and sulfides of copper. This causes it to work both on your heart center to make you open to the good possibilities, and also on your vital energies that will allow you to pursue them when they come your way. Its rich green color connects it with all things green and fertile and it has an earthy energy that helps you manifest your desires in the here-and-now.

Tiger's-eye is a powerful stone generally used to bring about materialization of one's desires. This can be used with any work where you want to see firm, solid results. It acts from moment-to-moment, helping you with your work on a continuous basis.

Short-Term Attraction

If you would like to concoct a formula for short-term attraction and fun, begin with an oil for wishes, such as **wisteria** or **violet**, add something with antidepressant properties that also encourages attraction and success, such as **orange blossom**, to give a lift to your spirits and a bounce to your step. This will also have the same effect on those who smell it on you. Combine this with **amber** for its attracting properties and **honey**, which draws both love and prosperity and promotes inner balance. Anoint a rose-colored candle with this formula while you focus on the kind of thing you wish to attract. You can also use it in bath salts before a night on the town.

Attraction Oil

- 4 parts **wisteria**—wishes, inspiration
- 4 parts **orange blossom**—attraction, magnetism, love

- 1 part **amber**—attraction, love, happiness
- 1 part **honey oil**—love, harmony, balance

Honey oil and amber are both very sweet. You may want to decrease the amount you use if this mixture is too sweet for you. This is fine as long as they are in it to some degree and in equal proportions.

Choosing a Charm for Short-Term Attraction

For attraction charms of any duration, it is a good idea to choose rose-colored stones. Rose is a color associated with the heart, with the vital energies of the physical body, and with romance and passion.

Pink kunzite acts to help the individual remain balanced while moving past personal barriers he or she may have to making real-time decisions where the heart is concerned. While there may be layers of self-limitation and doubt that get in the way, a charm of pink kunzite can help the individual lay these aside and act in the moment to relate to circumstances in a positive way. It encourages self-confidence and a feeling of personal safety and security that can make acting in the moment for positive results possible.

Pink tourmaline resonates with both the heart and the passions to open the individual for playfulness and romance. Just as green tourmaline can be used with fast luck, pink tourmaline acts quickly for fast playful attraction.

Charging Objects for Short-Term Work— Blessing a Space or Pursuit

If you wish to bless small objects or quick enterprises, such as short journeys or a weekend yard sale, you do not need to pull out all the big guns of a complete blessing, which is what you would do at the Full Moon. Blending an oil with a lighter fragrance can bring all the power and energy you need for a lighter task. This formula is a variation of a traditional blessing formula. Begin with **frankincense** to banish barriers and to bless, and add **myrrh** to transform all energies connected with the enterprise or object to the intention of its purpose. Myrrh banishes negativity and barriers, and acts to bring success to whatever purpose you intend. Add a light touch of **rose** as the final ingredient to assist the myrrh in its transformative capacity and to gently bless and consecrate whatever you wish. As with all formulas made at this time, you may blend the oil and charge it with your intention, then put it away for use at whatever Moon phase you may need it.

Light Blessing and Protection Oil

- 🖎 2 parts **frankincense**—banishes negativity and barriers, protects, consecrates
- 🖎 2 parts **myrrh**—transforms energy, protects, strengthens, banishes negativity, brings material gain, success
- 🖎 1 parts **rose**—transformative, consecrates

Healing, Calming, and Restoring

This is a good time of the month to do healing work. The shadows brought by the Dark of the Moon may be more lingering in some people. Traditionally, the dark phases of the Moon are more conducive to illness, so restoration and regeneration may be the order of the day. Any formula you use should include elements that are antidepressant. A strong spirit is as powerful in fighting disease and malaise as any medicine. Your formula should also include elements that are regenerative and restorative. Depending on the nature of the problem, you can extend this oil into incense to clear a stuffy sickroom and banish the energies of infirmity and illness, or into bath salts if the problem calls for soaking out mental, emotional, or physical ailments in the tub.

For general healing energy and to clear a sickroom, you can start with a combination of equal portions of **vetivert** and **spikenard**. Vetivert renews and encourages regeneration of body and spirit among its many other properties of increase and strength. Spikenard was greatly valued by the ancients and was said to have been one of the gifts brought to King Solomon by the Queen of Sheba. It is a specific strengthener for the heart center as well as a powerful agent to increase general health and vitality. You can lighten and balance this combination with **lemon verbena**. It has the same antidepressant and spirit-lifting properties as the citrus family but harmonizes better with the rich earthy tones of the vetivert and spikenard. It also has powers of hex-breaking that, in this application, can be powerful to disperse the miasma of sickness and weakness that often pervades a sickroom.

Sickroom Clearing Oil

- 2 parts **vetivert**—strength and regeneration
- 2 parts **spikenard**—health, harmony, balance
- I parts **lemon verbena**—happiness, uplifting, hex-breaking

Healing is a broad topic, and it is up to you to determine the nature of the help that the situation calls for. If the problem is mental or emotional rather than physical, your choice of ingredients will need to be appropriate to the situation. The Mental Clarity formula can work well in the case of depression as well as in times of extreme emotion. **Lavender** is one of the most powerful of all scents for restoring balance and harmony within the individual. When it is combined with **angelica**, it assists in bringing about inner peace and balance, because the angelica is a strong agent to dispel inner negativity, restore the mental and emotional systems, and help release any residual effects that may be lingering.

Choosing a Charm for Healing, Calming, and Restoring

When doing healing work, it is always a judgment call as to whether the individual in question needs an energy boost or more peace and quiet. If energy is what is called for, the yellow and orange stones we have already discussed will work quite well for this, too. If they need peaceful restoration, peaceful green stones and frosty white ones will work very well.

Jade is sometimes called the Stone of Peace. It acts through the emotional body to bring the wearer a sense of peace and balance. Its green nature is a good restorative for whatever energies are flagging and in need of support. It helps the wearer to find an inner sense of being loved and nurtured.

Milky quartz is also known as white quartz. It has a peaceful, soothing nature and will act on all the energy systems of the body to integrate and balance the energy systems. It is highly restorative, but in a gradual and gentle way acting to bring energies that have been overtaxed back into harmony with natural healthy levels.

Chapter 5

This is the time when the Moon's energy is at its peak and provides us with the power to work magic that can lead to a complete transformation of our lives and circumstances. This is the gateway to transition where we can firmly set our path into the lives we wish to create. The Full Moon generates the energy of expansion and creativity, allowing us an excellent opportunity to create our lives as we would wish them to be. This phase is represented by the fully mature Goddess, ripe with nurturing and possibilities. Now is the phase when work can be done for love magic to bring love and relationships into your life, and prosperity and abundance to you; to bring the circumstances that will ensure long-term material increase; to bring new opportunities that will change the direction of your life, and to align with specific energies and archetypes; and to bring lasting spiritual growth and change to your heart, and to magnify your spiritual path. The elements and oils you choose for this work will be different from the ones used at the Waxing Moon. At that time, you were working for short-term results. Now you are working to reset the matrix of circumstances and the oils and spells will be stronger and work on many more levels.

Remember that the ground must be prepared for the transformative process to be effective. There must be a space made in your life for the new situations to manifest themselves. If you have not cleared the way, then there may not be room for such changes to take place. Or if they do, they will become entangled with the old and not manifest in the way you want them to. You should remember, however, that transition is a complex process and does not happen overnight. It is an ongoing process of transformation that should unfold as you move into your work. If you truly wish a change in your circumstances, you cannot sit quietly at home waiting for change to come to you. When change presents itself, you must be willing to explore and pursue it, taking advantage of new situations as they come into your life. This is very important. The best magical work ever done will go for nothing if it is not backed up by real work to manifest the energies on this physical plane.

Work done at the time of the Full Moon is often more successful if it is done in a structured and formal way. Things can be undertaken casually while the Moon waxes because the results are intended to be transient and light. But if you call for things to be of a permanent nature—serious changes in how things are with you—then you need to take time in both preparation and execution. Your work should take place in a peaceful ritual setting with candles and incense in place. All the elements should be represented and the Spirit element—your letter of intent—should have been thought through and carefully written. Working at the Full Moon means creating the type of situation you would like to see come about. As the Moon darkens, its energy will carry away the residual of circumstances and forces that have been standing in your way.

Love, Attraction, and Passion

During the Waxing Moon, your love and attraction work had more to do with flirtation and having a fun time than the prospect of a lasting and meaningful relationship. During the Full Moon, however, your work can take on a deeper quality to reach for the kind of relationship you truly want in your life on a long-term basis. Begin with a base of **orange blossom** or any fragrance that has strongly magnetic attraction qualities combined with attributes of love and attraction. Add **jasmine**, which combines love of the sensual kind with love of the spiritual kind. Jasmine attracts all kinds of material increase and abundance, and encourages security and happiness. Next add **honey** oil. Its rich, heady scent also attracts love of the heart, the Spirit, and the senses. Finish the blend with **rosewood** for its connection to higher spiritual powers and its aura of peace and balance.

Make this blend into bath salts and incense to do a complete ritual wish spell. Use a rose seven-day candle anointed with the formula as your center light. Wear the oil in a scent carrier around your neck until the candle burns out.

Love-Seeking Oil

- 4 part **orange blossom**—love (long-lasting), sensuality
- 2 part **jasmine**—love, abundance, material and spiritual happiness
- 1 part **honey**—sensuality
- 1 part **rosewood**—peace, higher awareness

Rose-Petal Beads for Love Magic

Roses have always been associated with the Blessed Virgin Mary, and the scent of roses accompanies the visions that many have had of her. It is said that when an Ave Maria is said in her honor, a rose is laid at her feet. To say a complete rosary is to make a crown of roses for her. Legend has it that in medieval times, ladies gathered the petals from their gardens and used them to make their prayer beads in honor of her, and that this is where the name *rosary* comes from. Flower-petal beads can be made from any flower whose petals are thick and have a good body to them and whose scent is carried strongly in the petals, such as **ylang-ylang**, **gardenia**, **frangipani**, and **magnolia**.

Roses are also associated with love—romantic, spiritual, and sensual. To make a goddess charm to draw love into your life, you can make a strand of rose beads. As you work the beads, focus on the kind of love you want in your life. As you wear them, their fragrance will constantly reinforce the power of your spell to you, and it will work subliminally on those around you. Mixing ylang-ylang petals in with the rose will add a sweet, clean overtone to their fragrance, making this a powerful charm for love on many levels.

Collect at least a gallon-jarfull of fresh rose petals. The color doesn't matter because they will turn black during the bead-making process. Dried petals will not work for this, so try to gather them all on the same day, if you can. Pick them early in the morning, when their scent is strongest. Simmer them in a cast-iron skillet on *very* low heat with a tablespoon of water and a few drops of the appropriately scented oil. The idea is to soften and blacken the petals. As you simmer them, break them up and keep them from clumping, until the mixture is smooth, forming the consistency of biscuit dough. When the dough has cooled enough to touch, roll it into small balls and thread them on clear monofilament fishing line. You may add a fastener if you like. As you make each bead, repeat to yourself the affirmation that is the central theme of your spell. See the results fully realized in your mind. When you wear the beads, they will form a circle of energy and completion wherever you go.

Hang the strand in a warm, dry place with good ventilation. (If they are poorly ventilated they will mildew.) In some damp climates, they may take weeks to harden and sometimes you may want to shorten the drying time by heating them in a very slow oven (no warmer than you would use if keeping bread dough while rising). If you have a gas oven with an old-fashioned pilot light, this is an excellent drying environment. Be aware that fishing line is nylon and will melt if the heat is too high, and oven temperatures vary so you might want to make a short test-strand to gauge just how your oven works on this. In the heat of summer, sun drying works well also, but it takes much longer and you will need to cover them with a light layer of gauze to keep dust from settling on them.

When you wear them, the warmth of your body will release the scent. If they grow old and lose their scent, you may revive them by placing the strand in a plastic bag with a few drops of the appropriate oil diluted with isopropyl alcohol or dypropylene glycol (a tablespoon of this will be plenty). If you have made beads using a mixture of different flower petals, be sure you write down what you have put into them so that when the time comes to refresh them, you can mix the appropriate scent of oils. The beads are porous and will absorb the scented oil. Make sure that you hang them to dry again before wearing them.

Choosing a Charm for Love, Attraction, and Passion

Rose beads make a beautiful and unique charm to wear for your love magic. If you prefer something simpler (either to make or to wear), you may choose any piece that prompts you to reinforce your intention in your work. Red and rose stones make a good choice for this, because both activate the passions while uniting them with higher spiritual vibrations. This is a good combination of energy to bring out in any working for long-term partnership. Passion is only the beginning of a union, whether it is the physical passion of lovers or passionate devotion to a cause, ideal, or goal, as in a business partnership. It requires long-term commitment and deep understanding to ensure that a relationship stands the test of time.

Ruby is a member of the corundum family, some of the hardest stones known, with the exception of diamond. This hardness means that its crystalline structure is very strong and dense, and will carry a lot of energy. It comes in a wide range of colors from pale pink to deep wine red/purple. It amplifies the vibrations of passion and desirability in the individual's energy pattern, making him or her more magnetic to the vibration of love he or she wishes to call into his or her life.

Rose quartz is strongly connected to the heart center as well as to the primal-life base center. It unifies these two energies, so it is a stone of passion as well as love. It has a peaceful nature and enhances the strength of the heart and the strength of the vibrations with which the individual calls the love essence energy into his or her life.

Tourmaline comes in all the shades and hues of the rainbow and often it combines colors in layers from the inside out so that when it is sliced across the crystal, the center is a distinctly different color from the outside. **Watermelon tourmaline** is rose red in the center and dark, rich green on the outside—just like a watermelon. The rose center connects both to love and passion and the green outside enhances this with life-affirming energy to renew and revitalize the entire energy structure. Because it is a tourmaline, it is its nature to react automatically to the wearer, giving him or her the strength of energy required from moment to moment. This makes a delightful love charm stone because it unifies the energies and lightens the Spirit.

Abundance and Prosperity

Most of us would like a little long-term security—the knowledge that our resources are steady and can be relied upon. The Full Moon is a wonderful time to work for changing your prosperity situation. If you are not making the kind of money that you would like or if your job has come to a dead-end and is no longer satisfying to you, then it is definitely time to make a change. If there are too many leaks and holes in your life through which your resources are escaping, it is time to move to a more positive way of living. This is a time to open up new lines of resources and to safeguard and optimize the ones you have that you would like to keep so that your flow of abundance is stable and adequate to whatever needs may come up.

Using a base of **pine**, **fir**, or **evergreen** brings in the energy of perpetual abundance. These trees are green and strong year-round, which is definitely an energy you want to relate to your resources. **Cinquefoil**'s "green" smell brings in good luck, powerfully breaking the bonds of inertia that have limited you in the past while encouraging the energy of material prosperity. **Cypress** also has a rich green smell. This old man of the swamps can live through even the darkest of rainy days and thrive on it. Its energy brings long duration to the spell along with deep strong roots to permeate all phases of your life. To add a note of floral lightness, add **jasmine**. It is a powerful conductor of prosperity and money, bringing abundance and material happiness from many quarters.

Long-Term Abundance Oil

- 4 parts **pine** or **evergreen**—perpetual abundance
- 2 parts **cinquefoil** (**five finger**)—green smell, breaking bonds, power, material prosperity, good luck
- 1 part **cypress**—survives rainy days (lives in deep water), ensures longevity and duration of the spell
- 1 part **jasmine**—wealth and material well-being, happiness

Choosing a Charm for Abundance and Prosperity

Malachite's earthy energy makes this an excellent choice for an abundance stone. As the individual removes whatever blocks he or she might have to achieving their goal, malachite holds the place open left by these limitations until they are replaced with the desired positive structures. Its earthy nature as an oxide of copper makes it an excellent tool to bring material well-being into physical manifestation.

Changing Your Life—Blessing Your Space

This is also an excellent time to *bless* and *consecrate* the space in which you are living. More than just a place to hang your hat and lay your head, the space you live in has a powerful effect on you every moment you occupy it. You may want to change your life, but unless the vibrations of your living and sleeping space concur with that purpose, they will constantly reinforce old negative patterns that have been in place all along. This is the time to put the seal on whatever "Spring cleaning" you have done through the Moon's darker phases. It is now time to bring in the light and bless your space for a new and more radiant purpose.

A good blend to use for this is a fuller version of the light blessing we used for the Waxing Moon's small projects. You may mix this up as an oil if you like, or make a mixture of the dry ingredients with **frankincense** and **myrrh** tears (as the chunks are called), **sandalwood** shavings, and crushed **bay** leaves. Sprinkle this mixture with **rose** oil and toss it thoroughly so that the rose essence permeates the blend. Then store it in a tightly sealed jar so that the oil will not dissipate. Burn this on a charcoal block so that the smoke creates a powerful smudge to fill the space. It will drive out any negativity while blessing and protecting the space. It evokes a feeling of well-being and lifting of spirits that will allow you to create life anew in your space. This works as well for a space that you have been living in for a while that you want to change, as well as for new quarters you have just moved into. If you are moving into an older home, it is ideal for resetting the space and clearing out any residual energy from previous tenants.

If smoke is not an option due to the limitations of some spaces, such as a dormitory or office building, mix up the oil and then dilute it into alcohol or dypropylene glycol to use as a mist or spray. If you do so, be sure that as you bless the room, you cover the windows and light sockets and switches, as well as any air vents—any means of ingress or egress from the space. When you are done, the space will be completely blessed, sealed, and prepared for the new energy you want to bring into it.

House-Blessing Oil

- 4 parts **frankincense**—banishes negativity and barriers, protects, consecrates

- 4 parts **myrrh**—transforms energy, protects, strengthens, banishes negativity, brings material gain, success
- 4 parts **sandalwood**—protection, harmony, balance
- 2 parts **bay**—protection, purification, hex-breaking, overcoming opposition, consecration
- 2 parts **rose**—transformative, consecrates

Charging a Guardian for Blessing Your Space

To complete your blessing work, you may want to charge something to stand as a guardian of your space. This can be anything from a statue that you keep on the shelf to a plaque you hang over the door. Whatever form you choose, it should be a solid object with enough structural integrity to maintain an energy charge and stand the test of time in physical durability. A wreath of flowers is generally not solid enough to fulfill either of these, but a bouquet of appropriately chosen herbs can add to the protection of your house or living space. Traditionally, this would include a sprig of **rosemary** both for protection and for bringing good luck and happiness. It may also include **basil** for consecration, harmony, and happiness; **lavender** for protection, love, and peace; and **bay** leaves for protection and good luck. Take sprigs of each herb and make them into a small bundle. Bind the bundle with red thread or yarn for power and protection and hang it over your door. Every Spring you should replace the bundle with a new one and renew your blessing charm.

If you wish to charge a solid guardian, complete the cleansing and blessing of your space. Then in the center of the central room, take your chosen guardian object and focus your intention on it. Place the entire force of your focus on making this object the focal point of power for your peace and protection. See the guardian as alive and containing a conscious Spirit that will vigilantly guard and protect your space even when you are far from home.

Courage of the Heart—Beyond Empowerment

There are times in nearly everyone's lives when it requires more than just a momentary uplifting of natural confidence. Sometimes situations have become so ingrained and entangled that it requires serious self-transformation before you can make the changes you want. The confidence and courage to act on one's dreams is as important as the dreams themselves. Painful, limiting situations need to be drawn to a conclusion. Circumstances must be changed in order to move onward and outward. Often an individual has been trapped in self-limiting beliefs about him- or herself for years. Self-doubt can be a crippling condition and can cause you to watch your opportunities pass you by. A powerful formula combined with strong ritual work and meditation can help you find your inner strength and belief in yourself that you need to change your life and surroundings.

Carnation is the central element of this blend. It is ruled by the Sun, and its fiery nature is a strong stimulant to release its emotionally healing potential. It strengthens, blesses, and protects you in the course of your personal transformation. **Cedar** is also a fiery element and adds to the carnation by having similar properties that are connected to material success and strength. **Redwood** empowers and strengths the Spirit, while **allspice** reinforces the strength of will you will need to make the changes necessary.

Courage of the heart is the final step of an entire cycle dedicated to your commitment to changing your life that should include a thorough house-cleaning during the darker phases of the Moon. Its results will be long lasting and it is likely you will see the effects of this process for months, if not years, after the process is complete.

Courage of the Heart Oil

- 1 part **cedar**—strength
- 2 parts **dragon's blood**—power
- 1 part **rose geranium**—confidence and courage
- 2 parts **redwood**—empowerment
- 7 parts **carnation**—strength
- 1 part **allspice**—strength of will

Choosing a Charm for Courage of the Heart

Pad parajah is the common name given to a pink-orange sapphire. Being akin to sapphire, it specifically connects to the throat center that is the center of will and intention. It is brilliant orange and, therefore, is directly connected to the belly center, where the seat of personal identity is carried. Its energy strengthens and protects the function of self-esteem, personal courage, and centered empowerment needed to go forward into the new.

Zincite, whose principal element is zinc, connects its energies with the belly center. Zincite directly addresses loss of confidence and self-esteem lost through early childhood abuse, neglect, or abandonment. It also addresses issues from past lives that activate these self-limiting considerations. Its virtues include intensifying the focus and willpower of the individual to help attain your goals.

Hemimorphite helps the wearer to reassert control over his or her life by helping put ego-based considerations aside to reveal the true basis of self-limitations and doubts. It helps the wearer assume conscious control over self-esteem and self-image by allowing him or her to see whether the perceived limitations are real or are shadow fears gathered from false perceptions about self-worth or negative images projected from others.

Diamond's focused strength can contribute greatly to your ability to pursue a situation and ride the winds of change as you move toward your inner transformation. After fear and self-doubt have been seen for what they are and put aside, the brilliance of a diamond can help you clarify your path to achieving your goal.

Spirituality and Inner Awakening

The Full Moon is also a time when you can reaffirm your spiritual path and open your heart and Spirit to the energies and archetypes that will assist you to develop and grow. This is an excellent time for self-initiation or dedication of any kind as this is the time that long-lasting commitment is easiest to initialize. You can begin this process by working a general ritual to open your heart and Spirit to the most positive influences to enter—to ask for a new and vital spiritual light to come into your life. Regardless of your path or religion, this opening can begin a time of rededication to an old path that may have seemed to become stale or it can open you to a revelation about a new spiritual path to begin.

When choosing oils to open spiritual channels, you not only want to connect to higher energies, you also want to maintain harmony and balance while doing so. So it is important to include at least one, if not more, elements of your formula that have that power. It is also a good idea to take into account the need for psychic protection. In this case we do not mean that there is a possibility of attack from negative influences. Rather, as this is an opening process, there is likely to be a need for a little "insulation" from the abrasive mundane energies that assault us constantly. As you open these channels, you are more likely to be sensitive to them than at other times. By combining **rosewood**, **spikenard**, and **sandalwood**, you achieve a strong combination of these properties with the added strength of Spirit provided by the spikenard connecting directly through the heart chakra. Spikenard is also a traditional element of sacred anointing.

Opening the Spirit Oil

- 2 parts **rosewood**—connection to higher energies, peace, psychic protection
- 1 part **spikenard**—anointing, heart chakra, commanding, harmony, balance, health, psychic protection
- 1 part **sandalwood**—spirituality, protection, wisdom, harmony, balance

Choosing a Charm for Spirituality and Inner Awakening

Clear quartz has come to be synonymous with crystal. Its pure transparent structure is made of silicon dioxide, and this allows it to resonate with all of the energy systems that encompass the individual—spiritual, physical, mental, and emotional. When you are working for inner transformation, quartz makes an excellent focus stone because it addresses the person as a unity of energies. It unifies the energies of whatever intention you put behind it in a balanced and harmonious pattern across all of the energy centers. This makes it ideal for use as a focus stone in spiritual work. Set it between two white candles so that it reflects and refracts their light for a meditation stone, or wear it as a charm to carry the benefit of your meditations throughout the day.

Chapter 6

etween the powers of the Dark Moon and the Full Moon is a transitory aspect between Earth, the Sun, and the Moon. This is called an eclipse—a time when all three heavenly bodies are perfectly aligned, creating a gateway through all three powers—the Sun as Creation, the Moon as Motivating Force, and Earth as Physical Manifestation. An eclipse of the Sun is caused when the Moon moves between Earth and the Sun, thus momentarily blocking out the Sun and projecting the Moon's shadow onto Earth. When this occurs, it causes an alignment of these two tremendously powerful but diametrically opposing energies—the Sun that drives away all darkness and shadows, and the Moon that is the essence of reflection and shadow itself. This combination is extraordinarily powerful when working for great change of any kind, as it creates a kind of energy gateway through which it is possible to bring precisely attuned energy that will suit your purpose.

A lunar eclipse is nearly as powerful as a solar one. This occurs when Earth moves between the Sun and the Full Moon, causing Earth's shadow to block out the Sun's light from the lunar surface. With Earth in direct line between these opposing powers, it creates an intense pull of energy that can be used in many creative ways. The moment of the eclipse creates a powerful gateway in which you can project your intention for great change in your life and circumstances. This is the time to initialize a major cycle of transformation in your inner life—changes that will transform what you are now into what you wish to become. An eclipse of the Sun is the time to work for material circumstances—change in living situation, abundance issues, personal identity, and power. An eclipse of the Moon is the time to work for changes in your inner life, and emotional and personal issues. Each type of eclipse is fast-moving and transient, and it would be a good idea to check for the exact time at which the aspect is at its fullest to do the final part of your work. But the moment of the true eclipse is only the culmination of the aspect. Your work for this time should begin at least two weeks earlier with periods of daily meditation and personal preparation. The power of an eclipse is not to be wasted on hasty ill-prepared work. Use this time to evaluate not only the circumstance you wish to change, but also their underlying causes. Look at your life and its repeating cycles of failure or limitation that have prevented such changes in the past.

This makes a month's worth of exerted intention from one Full Moon to the next. Use the time preceding the Full Moon to align yourself with your objective by performing a daily or nightly cycle of meditation and journal work. Let your purpose become very clear in your mind. Work through its process with analysis in your journal. Make the image clear in your mind of exactly the results you wish to see. This is the cycle of time you should use to make any pictures or craft any charms you wish to create with the energy of the eclipse. Perform the design and fabrication work as a part of your preparation process. The actual tuning and charging should be a part of the eclipse ritual. For the two weeks after the eclipse, this charm should be worn as constantly as possible as you align yourself with the results and direction of the work.

Past-Life Awareness—Soul Retrieval

There are times in life when we encounter extremely traumatic and painful situations. This may be the result of intentional abuse at the hands of someone else, or it may be the result of a serious loss or injury due to an accident. The list of causes may vary, but the result is that we may have abandoned a part of ourselves in a moment that is too painful for us to assimilate at the time. These are turning-point stages of the personality, and in order to regain our wholeness, it may be necessary to return to those fragments of ourselves and welcome them back into the wholeness of our consciousness. This is not always easy because these fragments contain elements of pain, guilt, and grief—the same reasons we left them initially—that we do not wish to retrieve. But the irony is that if we do not retrieve them and reconcile them within the greater wisdom of our conscious mind, they will forever remain in the shadows of our psyches, crying and wailing, holding the load of grief that they cannot put down. The truth is that only by confronting an issue and dealing with it can you come to terms with it and lay it to rest. Just as when we get a splinter in our hand, digging it out may be painful and frightening, but failing to do so will only result in infection and further pain, and the final removal will be just as painful as if we had avoided all the complications and did it immediately.

These events may be in the present lifetime or may have occurred sometime in the far past when the Spirit inhabited a different body. There has been a great deal of discussion about past lives and reincarnation and the concept of *karma* that drives this cycle. Some people believe that they have lived before, sequentially life after life through time; others do not. In truth, past-life memories could be just that or they may be the subconscious mind's way of trying to work out a situation that is troubling or suppressed much in the same way we do when we dream.

As a part of your evaluation process, you may wish to include a cycle of past-life meditations. This may be done at any cycle from the Waning through the Dark of the Moon, but the cycle of working through the eclipse is the most powerful time of all for this type of process. All the elements—the Moon of the Inner Life, the Sun of the Exterior Life, and the Earth that represents the manifested reality of their influence—are present and aligned, acting upon each other more powerfully than at any other time. This is a powerful process that will address the roots of your limitations and negative cycles. There are several ways in which the past-life memories of your Spirit can be addressed—self-hypnosis, meditation, and guided journey to name just a few. Whichever method suits your personal working style, it is helpful to blend an oil to empower the work.

As a base for this formula, you will need oils that will enhance the clarity of your spiritual vision so that the information you gather will be specific and sharp—easily grounded in the rational thought process. **Mugwort** makes an excellent choice for this as it specifically opens the visionary process and enhances clarity. Added to this you need something that will protect your inner Spirit from undue outside negativity. Regression and past-life work can be a delicate time for you, and this kind of protection is important so that your work is not prejudiced or compromised by outside influences. **Myrrh** works very well for this purpose. Blended in equal parts with the mugwort, it will make a good foundation for your spiritual bridge into your own sub-conscious motivations. This sort of work also takes great personal and spiritual strength. It is not easy to see those events that were so traumatic that they are still affecting you after hundreds or thousands of years—events that were so difficult that they have carved deep scars on the spirit. Using **clove** will open these channels more easily so that you can do the work you intend to do, while combining it with **thyme** will add the strength you need to see it through. As a final note, adding **lotus** will stimulate the crown chakra, which will align you with your Higher Self so that you can work for your highest spiritual benefit. Be advised, however, that this is a powerful formula. Mugwort oil is a eu-phoric and can cause vivid dreams and visions, and can be mildly intoxi-cating. You should work with this formula in a protected space until you are certain how it affects you and you know what to expect from it.

Past-Life Regression Oil

- 4 parts **mugwort**—visionary clarity
- 4 parts **myrrh**—spiritual protection during the process
- 6 parts **clove**—opens everything
- 6 parts **thyme**—strength through courage
  or I part **allspice**—strength of Spirit
- 8 parts **lotus**—crown chakra

Blend 4 parts each of mugwort and myrrh for a base. Then add 6 parts each of clove and thyme. If you prefer, add the clove oil, but instead of using thyme oil, add a fresh sprig of thyme to the oil bottle and let is steep for a while. If you do not have fresh thyme, you may use the dried herb but crush it in your palm before you add it. When the first four ingredients are thoroughly mixed, add 8 parts of lotus oil to finish.

An alternative to this recipe would be to exchange the thyme for I part of allspice. Allspice brings in great strength of Spirit, but a little goes a long way. One part is all you would need to give it a rich, spicy aroma.

The two weeks after the eclipse are the period when the seeds of change will begin to expend powerful roots. You may have vivid or unsettling dreams. Unusual situations may arise with which you need to deal. This is the initialization of powerful forces as you have directed them to make substantial long-term changes in your life. It is understandable that you will begin to feel the effects of these changes on many levels of your life, although the ways they manifest may be subtle or surprising. These two weeks are as important as the previous ones because you will be guiding, directing, and affirming your energies and focus to make sure this beginning is as clear and precise as it needs to be. You have set a powerful machine into motion. This is no time to let it run on its own.

As the eclipse is a time to initialize long-range changes, you may not see concrete shifts immediately. Nonetheless, the magnitude of the work over the ensuing months may surprise you and eventually show results far beyond those you could have predicted. It is important to be mindful that your world is in a state of flux, and while the long-term results may be surprising, they are nonetheless part of the process you personally crafted and set to work.

As with any magical work, this work must take place in two areas—one is the external area of what results you wish to receive, the other is what preparation you do within yourself to make receiving this possible. This is vision work that centers on opening yourself to allow the energy of this special moment to flow into you, to fill you, and then to transform your situation. As time goes on, it is important to remember this and have faith in your own magical process. Do not fight the changes. Rather, be aware of them and continue guiding your life towards your determined goal. Always remember that your life is in a process of ongoing creation. The magic you do is a tool for your own growth that enables you to shape your life and future.

Choosing a Charm for Past-Life and Soul Retrieval Work

Amazonite (blue-green) is closely associated with the Egyptian god Anubis who is the guardian and guide of the Spirit, traversing all the dark places of the soul. This stone acts to knit back together any energy rifts and personal fragmentation caused by excessive trauma. It acts on mental and emotional levels together and is easily guided by the wearer. Once you have been through a regression process, it can be extremely helpful to integrate the information you have gathered. Its soothing nature helps you forgive both yourself and others while assimilating the larger patterns of events and interactions.

Ruby in zoisite is a powerful stone in personal transformation work. It has the unique power to reintegrate and fuse parts of the Spirit that have become alienated from the individual through trauma or neglect. It is also an invaluable tool if you are intending any serious cycle of past-life regression and soul retrieval. The ruby crystals give the inner strength and focus necessary to go to the heart of the issue, while the zoisite they are embedded in comes immediately behind it with a peaceful energy that knits up and resolves the issues that have been dealt with. Having this healing energy is highly beneficial. It literally reweaves the spirit into healthy patterns and, as a side benefit, brings closure and inner resolution so that you are less likely to replace old troubles with new ones as a way of filling the void left by any serious release.

The Power of the Planets

Chapter 7

*H*umankind has always had a fascination with the stars. The brilliant lights that illuminate the night sky have sparked endless speculation among both scientists and poets who conjecture on their nature and purpose and humankind's relationship to them. They move from hour to hour and season to season in a seemingly divine clockwork dance that provides a nightly light show of beauty and mystery. Babylonian astronomers were the first to record their observations that some of the lights in the sky moved differently than others. Sometimes the relative speed of their movements gave them the appearance of moving backwards in relationship to one another. Generations of careful observation led these ancient astronomers to conclude that when these planets were in certain positions in the sky, certain events were likely to occur on Earth. By analyzing their positions at the time of the birth of an individual, certain personality and behavioral traits could be predicted, and even potentially future events in that individual's life. From Babylon, the practice spread throughout India, Egypt, and the West, where it developed into two branches of study—Astronomy and Astrology. These early scientists observed that each planet seemed to have its own unique effect on earthly events and personalities, and so they ascribed each one to a deity who had the same traits.

The planetary energies have served humanity for eons as a way to express and describe particular qualities and powers of energies, existing in a heavenly or "otherworldly" form. Many peoples and cultures throughout history and around the world have named these planets for the gods and goddesses of their religion, to classify the powerful higher energies that rule human destiny to these remote heavenly lights. In English we call the planets by the names of gods and goddesses in the Greek pantheon. We know them as archetypes because they directly embody the basic elements of human life and behavior. They represent an ideal of a particular quality of energy.

There are seven major celestial bodies that can be observed with the naked eye, which were studied extensively in ancient times—Sun, Moon, Mercury, Venus, Mars, Jupiter, and Saturn. The ancient astronomers referred to all of them as "planets." They are put in this order because this is how they appear from Earth, as though Earth were the center of the solar system. Even though science has known otherwise for a long time, both in an astrological and arcane sense, they are still counted in the old order. There are also three more planets that have only been known to us since relatively recent times— Neptune, Uranus, and Pluto. Since their discovery, their qualities have also been identified and have been added to the lists of powers. The planets symbolize and/or embody specific categories of energy and also correspond to many other symbols, concepts, and forces. For thousands of years, the planets have served as a means to personify and categorize the conditions of our existence, our needs, and the forces operating in our lives as a way to better focus on them, understand, and, perhaps, to deal with them.

In a magical process, there is something more important to consider than the perfume quality of the scents you are choosing, and that is the quality of the energies that they represent. This purpose of blending the right formula of oil for your work is intended to trigger your energies to align with the energies of your goal or purpose. Everything in nature has a particular energy quality of its own that defines its nature. Herbs and their scent have been identified for hundreds of years not only for how they smell, but by what the smell invokes. One way we describe this energy property is to say that a certain herb is "under the rulership" of a particular planet. It is not necessary to become an expert on astrology to use this classification guide. But it is a good idea to understand a little about the powers of the planets to broaden your understanding of the powers of the herbs they rule. When we look at a list of oils to select them for a specific property, we must also look at their planetary rulers. Besides the element under which they fall, their planetary rulers define the nature of their behavior and the specific ways in which they work. For example, many oils fall under the element of Fire, but the ones ruled by the Moon will address their fiery activity through the emotions; the ones ruled by Mercury will address the same issues, but through the mind; the ones ruled by the Sun will address the outward expression of their properties; and so on.

Sun ☉

Outer Person
Illumination
Metal: Gold
Color: Orange
Element: Fire
Chakra: Belly

The Sun is the ruler of outward appearances and of shedding light on what was obscured by darkness. In Greek mythology, Apollo was the driver of the fiery Sun chariot as well as the patron of the Delphic Oracle. Astrologically, the Sun rules the public personality—the extroverted side of the individual. Apollo was also the patron of healers; healing in the sense that hidden causes of disease and disorder were driven out. The Egyptian lion goddess, Sekhmet, was associated with the fiery burning principle of the Sun and was credited with the power not only to destroy the world and bring disease and plague, but also to drive out the demons of pestilence and to defend and uphold the Universal order. She was also considered the patroness of healers.

The Sun corresponds with the warrior chakra of the belly. His illumination is the defense and protection against the powers of darkness and ignorance, and will guard the personality—the Self. He is the bringer of truth because he drives out the shadows of deception. But be cautious about what you expose to his light. There is an old story about the boy, Icarus, whose father made him wings from feathers and wax. He flew magnificently through the sky, freed from prison and darkness, but he forgot to heed his father's warning. When he flew too near the Sun, the wax holding the feathers together melted, and Icarus crashed to Earth and was killed. The power of light and fire is double-edged, and you should be aware of what you are asking when you call the Sun's energy to act in a situation.

The Sun is the sign of the victor, and rules power and success, executives, and employers. Its influence is invoked to bring light into shadows and darkness, and to gain the favorable notice of people in high places. The Sun's metal is gold, and its stones are golden ones, such as amber, and orange ones, such as citrine and carnelian.

Herbs ruled by the Sun are those that illuminate the heart and drive away the shadows of doubt, sickness, and negativity.

Acacia	Frankincense	Orange
Angelica	Grapefruit	Orange Blossom
Bay	Heliotrope	Orange, Mandarin
Bergamot	Honey	Peony
Carnation	Honeysuckle	Rosemary
Cinnamon (Cassia)	Hyacinth	Rosewood
Citronella	Hyssop	Safflower
Citrus	Juniper	Saffron
Civet	Marigold	Sesame
Cloves	Mistletoe	Tangerine
Cranberry	Myrrh	Tuberose
Evergreen	Olibanum	Walnut

Moon ☽

Inner Self
Healing and Intuition
Metal: Silver
Color: White
Element: Water
Chakra: Crown

Just as everyone has an outward-facing "daytime" side that is visible to everyone around us, we also have an inner, secret side that is not seen, and is only visible through its reflections, such as moods and behavior. As the Sun corresponds to our outward face, the Moon (that is never seen by its own light, but only by reflected light) rules the inner person and its expressions as feelings, intuitions, visions, and dreams. It also rules the home and family, which are the expressions of the inner private person as opposed to one's public face.

Magical Oils by Moonlight

The Moon is associated with all things governed by or in rhythm with its forces, such as the tides and waters, and the female reproductive cycles and organs. By extension, it also rules issues concerning children.

Whether you are seeking inner healing or working to expand and broaden your intuition and perception of the larger world, Moon energy is part of that pattern. The Moon offers nurturing and guidance, and is said to rule both mothers and teachers. Seek Moon energy when you feel the need for inner healing, when you feel entrapped by your life or unable to solve a tangled problem. Moon energy rules intuition and inner guidance, and can open up your inner vision to new avenues of solutions and opportunities; because of this connection, it is ascribed to the crown chakra.

There are many practitioners who say that because the Moon rules this inner world and the connection to higher wisdom, it should be considered when doing any working of power. It is important to consider what phase the Moon is in. The growing, or Waxing, phase is said to be most powerful for drawing things to the individual; for making things come about; and for work concerning healing, fertility, and increase in general. When it is growing thinner, Waning, it is the time for removing things and severing ties. There is an old gardener's saying that you should weed your garden and pull up stumps when the Moon is waning so that they won't come back. This is also the case in a wider scope of activity. A good example of how this works would be if you were working for abundance, more financial plenty, and security. When the Moon is Waxing or Full, work for all this bounty and/ or the ability, knowledge, and opportunity necessary to attain or achieve it. When the Moon is Waning or Dark, work to have poverty and the barriers to abundance removed, for the banishing of ignorance, lack of resources, and bad luck.

Just as the Moon has many aspects or faces, so are its attributes personified by many different deities—the goddesses Artemis/Diana (the virgin huntress), Hecate (dark goddess of magic), and Isis (in both her capacity as Divine wife and mother and her role as mistress of magic). The Moon in its three visible phases is also used to describe and symbolize the Triple Goddess—Maiden, Mother, and Crone—power and self-sufficiency for the virgin huntress (Maiden), creativity and fertility for the Mother, and wisdom for the Crone.

The Moon's metal is silver. It rules all white and milky stones, such as moonstones, white star sapphires, opal, and diamond, and watery ocean stones, such as pearl, mother-of-pearl, and coral.

Herbs ruled by the Moon have the qualities of her nature both as ruler of women's mysteries and as mistress of the night. Herbs include relaxants, soporifics, and those that pertain to female natural cycles. The Moon also rules creatures of the element of Water, and so the list includes lotus and water lily, as well as the liquid-filled coconut.

Camellia	Hibiscus	Poppy
Camphor	Jasmine	Raspberry
Chamomile	Lemon	Sandalwood
Coconut	Lemon-Lime	Water Lily
Gardenia	Lotus	
Grape	Oakmoss	

Mercury ☿

Messenger
Metal: Brass/Mercury
Color: Yellow
Element: Air
Chakra: Solar Plexus

Mercury is the winged messenger of the gods, and as such, he rules short journeys and swift communications. He deals with all writings, authors, and record-keeping, and, therefore, schools and research. His qualities are eloquence and intelligence—all capacities of the intellect. He is also known as the Opener of Ways, who carries prayers to the gods and their messages to humankind. But his influence is not always obvious. He is a trickster and a thief, and there are many stories associating him with pranks and thefts; therefore, he rules covert activities, thieving, and spying. By this, it is meant that only through opening our intelligence to new ways of thinking can we achieve what we desire.

In his role as messenger, he is called Mercury/Hermes; as record-keeper and guide, Thoth/Anubis; as trickster and thief, Coyote/Loki. It is interesting to note that as a trickster, he is often involved in pranks that teach the victim by pointing out faults in planning or purpose, or fatal flaws of character from which the victim can learn and grow. In effect, he trips us with our own untied shoelaces in order to make a point.

Mercury corresponds to the solar plexus chakra, the Dancer, and refers to our inner center of personal balance. He opens the ways for self-knowledge. Mercury reminds us that when our own inner harmony is out of tune, nothing will go very far or very well. The work that we do will be the reflection of our imbalance. The metal of Mercury is quicksilver or brass, and its stones are neutral-colored ones, such as onyx or agate.

Herbs ruled by Mercury are those that enliven and brighten the mind to increase mental acuity.

Almond	Clary Sage	Marjoram
Anise	Clover	Mint
Azalea	Crab Apple	Peppermint
Balsam, Fir	Lavender	Snowdrops
Bayberry	Lemon Grass	Valerian
Blue Bonnet	Lily of the Valley	Wintergreen
Caraway	Mandrake	

Venus ♀

Beauty and Pleasure
Metal: Copper
Color: Green/Rose
Element: Water
Chakra: Heart/Base

In many cultures, the planet Venus is associated with the Queen of Love and Beauty; as such, she embodies the aesthetic, the fertile, and the erotic. She is the source of passion. She is the mistress of all pleasures and beautiful things as well as the people who create them—music and musicians, art and artists, and, of course, love and lovers.

Venus rules the heart and emotions and the creative and generative forces that come from it. As physical and romantic love unites male and female, and leads to the procreation of children, it is the passion of Venus that unites the opposing qualities in ourselves to create and bring forth the manifestation of our highest dreams to reach toward the future. It is Venus who guides the hand of the artist to bring abstract concepts into concrete reality. She represents the fertility and bounty of any project, and, consequently, represents money and wealth of all kinds.

The metal of Venus is copper, and her stones are green ones, such as emeralds, jade, moss agate, and malachite.

Herbs of Venus are those that increase beauty, attract admiration, and encourage love and passion.

Allspice	Dove's Blood	Pikake
Almond	Frangipani	Plumeria
Althea	Freesia	Primrose
Amber	Geranium	Rose (Red, White,
Apple Blossom	Green Apple	Wild, Yellow)
Apricot	Heather	Spearmint
Aster	Lemon Verbena	Strawberry
Banana	Lilac	Sweet Pea
Benzoin	Magnolia	Sweetgrass
Birch	Mugwort	Thyme
Burdock	Musk	Tulip
Calamus	Orchid	Vanilla
Catnip	Orris	Verbena
Cherry	Papaya	Vervain
Cherry Blossom	Passion Flower	Vetivert
Cyclamen	Peach	Violet
Damiana	Pennyroyal	Wisteria
Dittany	Persimmon	Ylang-Ylang
Dogwood		

Mars ♂

Warrior
Metal: Iron
Color: Red
Element: Fire
Chakra: Base

Mars/Ares is the fiery red planet of the warrior energy, ruling all things that are fiery, warlike, and aggressive. Mars energy is not simply the quality of destruction and combat, it is aggressive and assertive energy as opposed to merely anger and violence. The forceful energy of Mars clears away obstacles to progress, achievement, and self-knowledge. Mars can destroy in order to renew, and in this aspect it rules surgeons, the police, and remodeling contractors. Egyptian lion-headed Sekhmet is a warrior goddess in her aspect as Destroyer of the Enemies of World Order. Assyrian Astarte (Ishtar), goddess of war as well as Queen of Love and Beauty in her chariot pulled by lions, and Hindu Durga/Ambaji on her tiger, are excellent examples of this dual energy. Mars rules sexual energy as it is expressed in the mating instinct—the drive to reproduce and defend the young.

Iron is the metal of Mars, and all red stones, such as jasper, garnet, and ruby are his as well.

Herbs ruled by Mars increase energy and aggression. They also encourage confidence and self-esteem.

Anemone	Ginger Blossom	Pine
Basil	Ginseng	Pineapple
Coriander	High John	Rose Geranium
Cumin	the Conqueror	Rue
Dragon's Blood*	Hollyberry	Tuberose
Galangel	Menthol	Wormwood
Ginger	Mustard	

(* In the older herbals, dragon's blood was attributed to Mars. Some of the newer ones give its rulership to Pluto.)

Jupiter ♃

Abundance/Nourishment
Metal: Tin
Color: Violet/Purple
Element: Earth
Chakra: Brow

The English words *jolly* and *jovial*, meaning "happy, joyful, and expansive," come from the Latin spelling for Jupiter, which is *Jove*.

Jove/Jupiter/Zeus rules abundance, growth, plenty, expansion and generosity, wealth, and prosperity of all kinds. He is in charge of speculation and money matters (increase of investments).

Jupiter is described as the Father of all the gods. In an allegorical sense, this means that this energy is the fount from which all the qualities and benefits of the others flow. He is associated with lightning and Divine justice. In his role as Zeus Thunderer, the lightning of Jupiter can be of great help in removing the negative effects associated with injustice, such as anger, fear, grief, powerlessness, self-doubt, and illness. By helping you through this tangle of negativity and self-imposed limitations, Jupiter leads you into expansion. Jupiter gives courage of the heart and a broader scope of vision, and it is this influence that can show you how to be brave and forthright to go out and achieve your highest potential. Like having a wise, powerful, and just father on your side, Jupiter will not do it for you, but he will show you how to do it yourself.

Jupiter's metal is tin, and his stones are blue or violet, such as amethyst and sapphire.

Herbs of Jupiter encourage prosperity and abundance as well as the joy of living well.

Agrimony	Citronella	Obeah
Anise	Copal	Sage
Balm of Gilead	Hyssop	Sassafras
Cedar (Cedarwood)	Linden	Zula-Zula
Cinquefoil (Five Finger)	Nutmeg	

Saturn ♄

Teacher
Color: Black/Indigo
Metal: Lead
Element: Air
Chakra: Throat

Saturn is sometimes known as Chronos, Father Time, who rules death, wills, and old things and people. Saturn is the teacher of the lessons of life that come with experience, including self-discipline, self-knowledge, common sense, and awareness of one's own limitations. It is the energy of Saturn that enables you to pull yourself together and get down to work, which is the energy of hard work and determination that underlies any success or achievement. The influence of Saturn is often misunderstood and is seen as gloomy, cynical, limiting, and pessimistic, but the truth is that much can be learned and much strength gained from this practical energy. Saturn also rules land in the sense of ancestral lands and legacies of real property, and as such, is also identified with Vesta, the Roman goddess of the hearth and home. Consequently, Saturn is invoked in workings for protection of the hearth, home, and private possessions. It is said that amulets of Saturn, hidden beneath the doorstep, will keep any evil from entering the home. Saturn also protects women in childbirth, because childbirth is the gateway between life and death for both mother and child.

Saturn's metal is lead and his stones are black, such as onyx, obsidian, jet, and black coral (although rulership of black coral is shared with the Moon), and indigo, such as lapis lazuli.

Herbs ruled by Saturn address issues of old age and death as well as those that deal with binding and constricting.

Asafetida	Ivy	Spanish Moss
Bindweed	Mimosa	Spikenard
Cypress	Morning Glory	Spruce
Eucalyptus	Patchouli	Yerba Santa
Hemlock		

Neptune ♆

Inspiration/Secrets
Metal: None specified
Color: Turquoise
Element: Water
Chakra: Thymus

As ruler of the ocean, Neptune presides over secrets and hidden things of all types. Similar to the Moon, the influence of Neptune is felt on the inner psyche rather than the exterior. These are the energies that bring inspiration as well as psychic powers, mystical visions, and the occult. Neptune rules the unconscious and is associated with things that induce unconsciousness and altered states such as anesthetics, opiates, drugs, and intoxicants, and the results of these things such as confusion, self-delusion, hallucination, addiction, and escapism. Mysterious and hidden things are in this purview, such as spying and secrets, along with their negative counterparts, fraud and deceit. Neptune also rules over submarines and deep-water oceanography.

Although no metal is associated with Neptune, its stones are turquoise in color, such as turquoise, hemimorphite, gem silica, and chrysocholla.

Herbs under the rulership of Neptune are Kelp, Opium, and Yula.

Uranus ♅

Curiosity/Invention
Metal: Platinum & Aluminum
Color: Opalescence
Element: Air

Uranus presides over inventions, curiosity and investigations, and by association, all things that are original and eccentric, such as inventors and theoreticians. He is associated with inventions of the modern age, particularly those having to do with electricity and electromagnetism. Uranus rules electrical devices, computers, telephones, airplane travel, power plants, and nuclear energy.

Uranus is associated with variable colored stones, such as opal. His metals are platinum and aluminum (although these are associated with Pluto as well). Uranus rules the herb Narcissus.

Pluto ♀

Regeneration/Obsession
Metals: Uranium and Radium
Associations: Unspecified

The energies of Pluto bring transformation, rebirth, degeneration, extremes, and transmutation. This is the force that brings transformation into our lives. It is up to us to decide how we deal with it. They are the refining forces of annihilation, transmutation, regeneration, and rebirth. These forces deal with life and death and how we face our destiny—whether we choose regeneration or degeneration. Pluto also deals with control and large controlling organizations. Because of its long orbit, this planet seems to bear more influence on society than on the individual.

Herbs ruled by Pluto are Ambergris and Birch. In the older herbals, dragon's blood was attributed to Mars. In some of the newer ones, its rulership is given to Pluto.

	Color	Metal	Stone	Chakra	Angel	Scent	Day of the Week
Moon	White	Silver	Moonstone/ Opal/ Beryl/ Pearl/	Crown	Gabriel	Lavendar/ Clary Sage/ Lime	Monday
Mercury	Yellow	Mercury/ Brass	Neutral/ Agate	Solar Plexus	Ophiel	Mint/ Bayberry/ Clary Sage	Wednesday
Venus	Green/ Rose	Copper	Emerald/ Jade/ Malachite	Heart/ Basal	Hagiel (Haniel)	Roses/ Sandalwood/ Ylang-Ylang	Friday
Sun	Orange	Gold	Amber/ Topaz/ Heliodore	Belly	Raphael/ Michael	Laurel/ Cinnamon	Sunday
Mars	Red	Iron	Ruby/ Garnet/ Bloodstone	Base	Khamael	Dragon's Blood/High John the Conquerer	Tuesday
Jupiter	Purple	Tin	Amethyst/ Lapis Lazuli	Brow	Tzadkiel	Myrrh/ Frankincense	Thursday
Saturn	Blue/ Black	Lead	Onyx/ Obsidian	Throat	Tzaphkiel	Sage	Saturday

The Moon in the Zodiac

As the Moon moves across the heavens, it passes through the different houses of the Zodiac. This is called *transitting*, and each passage lasts about three days. Depending on the quality of the Zodiac sign it is passing through, these transits energize the power of the Moon, and trigger the behavior and events that then become a part of your daily experience. It is as though the Moon is putting a magnifying lens to each in turn, and bringing these powers into focus in your life and work. When doing any kind of magic, you can increase the power of what you are doing by using the almanac to find the sign whose powers best relate to the purpose you have in mind and waiting until the Moon is in that sign to do your work.

Aries

Element: Fire
Ruler: Mars
Color: Red
Stone: Ruby, Bloodstone

Those born in the sign of the Ram are independent and active—forceful, dynamic, brave, and self-assured. They love challenges and are born pioneers. Work in the sign of Aries when you need to break through barriers and forge into unknown territory, and when you need the Mars warrior energy on your side. Aries favors fire magic.

Taurus

Element: Earth
Ruler: Venus
Color: Green
Stone: Emerald

Those born in the sign of the Bull are loyal and generous. They love security, appreciate the good things in life, and are not afraid of working to get them. They are gracious and romantic. Work in the sign of Taurus when seeking abundance and material well-being. Its Venus energy is also beneficial when doing love magic to draw a long-term lover to your side, and will bless the match with security and comfort. This sign favors success in business and seeking employment.

Gemini

Element: Air
Ruler: Mercury
Color: Yellow
Stone: Topaz

Those born in the sign of the Twins are witty and talkative. They are said to have a dual nature that can do several tasks at once. They delight in diversity and change. Work in the sign of Gemini when initiating new ventures to make sure your transition doesn't miss any details and is smooth. Gemini will also help with seeking new employment and in any venture that requires eloquence and sharp wits, including scholarship and research. It is good to address mental health issues under this sign.

Cancer

Element: Water
Ruler: Moon
Color: Silvery Pastels
Stone: Moonstone, Pearl

Those born under the sign of the Crab can be shy and sensitive, as well as nurturing and tenacious. They are natural nurturers and teachers. They are great lovers of hearth and home, and prize tradition and heritage. Work in the sign of Cancer for enterprises that require tenacity to bring long-term rewards. This is also a favorable sign for love magic when seeking a partner who is nurturing and supportive. Because it is ruled by the Moon, magic involving the welfare of children can be undertaken under this sign. Cancer can help bring order into your life.

Leo

Element: Fire
Ruler: The Sun
Color: Gold, Orange
Stone: Carnelian

Those born under the sign of the Lion are theatrical and outgoing, proud of their achievements, chivalrous, and noble. They are great lovers of display and pleasure. Work in the sign of Leo for all undertakings regarding performing, public recognition, fame, and glory. This is a good time to open a stage show or start an advertising campaign. This is also a sign to work under when situations require control and defense.

Virgo

Element: Earth
Ruler: Mercury
Color: Blue, Gray
Stone: Jacynth

Those born under the sign of the Maiden are analytical and careful, organized and efficient. Their standards are high for both themselves and others. They are compassionate and respond to those in need. Work in the sign of Virgo to bring precision and organization to your purpose. Virgo also favors setting up housekeeping and establishing organizations. This is a good sign to work to solidify friendship.

Libra

Element: Air
Ruler: Venus
Color: Rose, Blue
Stone: Rose Quartz, Chrysocholla

Those born in the sign of the Balance are peace-loving, just, and eloquent. However, their search for balancing everything sometimes makes them seem indecisive. Work in the sign of Libra to bring order and harmony to any situation. This is the sign to work under for legal matters when seeking justice and the righting of wrongs.

Scorpio

Element: Water
Ruler: Pluto
Color: Red, Black
Stone: Garnets

Those born under the sign of the Scorpion are passionate and energetic. They are complex, contradictory, and many layered.

Sometimes difficult to know, they are loyal and warm to those they love. Work under the sign of Scorpio to evoke passion. This sign also favors spying, deceit, and all things requiring subtlety and working behind the scenes. It is favorable for divorce and severance work, and also to bring the wayward back home.

 ## *Sagittarius*

Element: Fire
Ruler: Jupiter
Color: Purple, Dark Blue
Stone: Amethyst, Sapphire

Those born under the sign of the Archer are forceful, dynamic, fun-loving, and optimistic. They are sometimes restless and often plain-spoken. Work under the sign of Sagittarius when hard work and determination are called for, especially on projects that will bring profit to all concerned. This sign can bring clarity and revelation in all matters.

 ## *Capricorn*

Element: Earth
Ruler: Saturn
Color: Dark Blues, Browns
Stone: Amber, Smoky Quartz

Those born under the sign of the Sea Goat are serious and single-minded. They are conscientious and determined in their pursuit of their goals. This is a good sign in which to cleanse and banish—especially when you are trying to break a habit. This sign has the power to break engrained energy patterns that have a negative effect. Work in Capricorn to do binding and limiting. This is the time to do karma magic.

 ## *Aquarius*

Element: Air
Ruler: Uranus
Color: Green, Bright Blue, Purple
Stone: Sapphire

Those born under the sign of the Water Carrier are idealists and dreamers. They have calm, pleasing, and agreeable temperaments. They have a natural sense of justice and fairness. Aquarius favors bringing dreams into reality, plans and projects, idealism, and artistic endeavors. This sign also favors remembering dreams and visions.

Pisces

Element: Water
Ruler: Neptune
Color: Green, Greenish Blue
Stone: Quartz, Opal, Aquamarine

Those born in the sign of the Fishes are imaginative, intuitive, introspective, and romantic. Pisceans are quiet and excellent keepers of secrets. Pisces favors metaphysical pursuits and psychic activity. Work under this sign to empower inner journeys, psychic development, and personal enlightenment.

Void of Course— Moon of Silence

The Moon's energy is receptive. She takes her light from the Sun and her "coloring," or energy, from the planets and signs, bringing emphasis to their powers through her focus. Sometimes the almanac tells us that there is a gap between the signs as the Moon passes through the Zodiac. This is a time when the Moon is on its way from one sign to another but is not fully in any sign. This time is called Void of Course or sometimes the *Moon of Silence*. When you are working for a specific objective, it is best to avoid such a time because the energy is insubstantial and non-directed. Plans can easily go awry or manifest in undesirable ways. This time occurs about every three days and can last from a few hours up to a day; you would be well advised to wait until the Moon enters a specific sign.

The general wisdom about Void of Course Moon is that the energy is unfocused and unproductive. This is a time when your thinking tends to be disorganized and plans that you make are incomplete or internally flawed. Consequently, you should avoid starting any new projects, or making important decisions or major purchases. This is not a good time to interview for a job or seek advice from anyone, especially a doctor or lawyer. Partnerships formed at this time tend to flounder. The best advice for this time seems to be to allow it to be a resting time when you take care of minor details and allow the energies to regroup themselves for the coming sign energy. This is a good time to rest and meditate.

However, when you are working to dispel, disperse, and banish unwanted energies from your life, Void of Course can be a good time to send these energies packing into the Void.

The Planetary Hours

If you wish to refine your timing still further, even the hours of the day have been ascribed to planetary rulers. By choosing days and times for your work ruled by the planets most favorable to your purpose, you can add this energy to the phase and sign of the Moon. By "ruled" we mean that the desired planet has its strongest influence at this time. By using an almanac, you can determine the exact time of sunrise and sunset in your area. Sometimes it is listed in your local newspaper. Although the day is 24 hours long, the time from sunrise to sunset is only precisely 12 hours on the Equinoxes. Determine the exact number of minutes between sunrise and sunset (or sunset and sunrise) and divide the total by 12. This will give you 12 even "hours" in which you can find the planetary ruler in the following chart. Because of the seasonal variance, these will not be 60-minute hours, but either longer or shorter, according to the season. Remember that sunset is considered to begin the first hour of the day. This may take a little getting used to. For instance, Sunday is actually considered to begin at sunset on Saturday; Monday begins at sunset on Sunday; and so on. A more precise way of working is to buy a Planetary Hour book. This gives precise astronomical charts to determine the exact hour of the day that the planets are at their strongest.

	Sunday	Monday	Tuesday	Wednesday	Thursday	Friday	Saturday
1st	☉	☽	♂	☿	♃	♀	♄
2nd	♀	♄	☉	☽	♂	☿	♃
3rd	☿	♃	♀	♄	☉	☽	♂
4th	☽	♂	☿	♃	♀	♄	☉
5th	♄	☉	☽	♂	☿	♃	♀
6th	♃	♀	♄	☉	☽	♂	☿
7th	♂	☿	♃	♀	♄	☉	☽
8th	☉	☽	♂	☿	♃	♀	♄
9th	♀	♄	☉	☽	♂	☿	♃
10th	☿	♃	♀	♄	☉	☽	♀
11th	☽	♂	☿	♃	♀	♄	☉
12th	♄	☉	☽	♂	☿	♃	♀

Hour After Sunset

Magical Oils by Moonlight

Hours After Sunrise	Sunday	Monday	Tuesday	Wednesday	Thursday	Friday	Saturday
1st	♃	♀	♄	☉	☽	♂	☿
2nd	♂	☿	♃	♂	♄	☉	☽
3rd	☉	☽	♂	☿	♃	♀	♄
4th	♀	♄	☉	☽	♂	☿	♃
5th	☿	♃	♀	♄	☉	☽	♂
6th	☽	♂	☿	♃	♀	♄	☉
7th	♄	☉	☽	♂	☿	♃	♀
8th	♃	♀	♄	☉	☽	♂	☿
9th	♂	☿	♃	♀	♄	☉	☽
10th	☉	☽	♂	☿	♃	♀	♄
11th	♀	♄	☉	☽	♂	☿	♃
12th	☿	♃	♀	♄	☉	☽	♀

The Elements of Magic

Chapter 8

*T*he ancient Greek sages theorized that the Universe we perceive with our physical senses is composed of five separate elements. Everything that we see or experience here can be described as a combination of varying proportions of the elements **Air**, **Fire**, **Water**, **Earth**, and **Spirit**. Although the science of our modern era has discovered a good many more elements and has redefined the way in which the physical Universe is structured, the five philosophical elements still remain a good way in which to conceive of the metaphysical elements of Creation. It can be said that all things that exist—at least in a theoretical sense—are some combination of the first four unified by Spirit, which defines and animates them. In another way, we can envision this Universe as composed entirely of Spirit, manifesting itself in endless combinations of the first four.

From another perspective, we can say that everything we see, touch, hear, smell, and feel is a manifestation of energy. When pure energy slows down, it condenses into increasingly solid forms of matter. The cycle of the elements is about how the four elements condense, moving slower and slower until they come together into a coherent structure—from invisible air, to insubstantial fire, to fluid water, and then into concrete earth. All things, whether they are objects, conditions, or ideas come into being in this way. Air represents potential, the basic ideal of a thing, condition, or plan. As yet, it has no form or direction, only the potential of the many things it could become. Fire represents the inspiration or action that begins to organize that potential into reality. Water represents its organization as it flows into solidity. The form is still not concrete, but tangible and containing its unique essence. Earth represents the final form and reality of the thing, its physical manifestation. The fifth element is the pattern or Spirit of that coherent structure—the way in which it is related to all other things. Spirit defines not only its singular identity, but also its identity as part of the continuum of Creation as a whole.

In a broader sense, the idea of the four elements unified by Spirit can be witnessed in conditions as well as things. The seasons of life, for example, can represent Air as Infancy, which is the potential of the individual; Fire as Childhood, in which the potential is shaped by action; Water as Adulthood, in which the action of Childhood bears its fruit; and finally, we reach Old Age, the culmination of the individual and the life's journey. All are unified by Spirit, that is, the identity or personality of the person regardless of age. The natural world of time and seasons can also be represented as the four elements in Dawn, Noon, Sunset, and Midnight, or Spring, Summer, Fall, and Winter, which are all unified by Time, the Spirit, or organizing principle, of the cycle itself.

As individuals, we are part of this cycle. We are Spirit manifesting in physical form. We contain a microcosm of the Greater Universe just as a drop of sea spray contains within it all of the elements of the great ocean. The presence of these elements within us connects us to the Greater Universe and all its unlimited potential. Like invisible cords, we are never separate from it and are always drawing upon its resources whether we are consciously aware of doing so. When we wish to change the condition of our lives or our consciousness, we have access to all these resources. We have but to put ourselves in tune with them and draw on the elements we wish to augment or diminish. The act of doing this is a process of literally adjusting our personal energies to correspond to the energies we wish to draw upon. Wish magic is the process of that attunement. We begin by literally changing ourselves.

Our gateway to this change is through our physical senses. It is an old truth that nothing can happen or exist in a Universe that does not obey the laws of that Universe. Regardless of the metaphysical or philosophical nature of what we are doing, we must remember that it is through a physical process that the results of our work will become real. We change our inner energies and attachments by using physical means to effect the changes we desire. Using smell, touch, taste, sight, and hearing, we act upon our energies to move ourselves into alignment with our objective. Besides giving us valuable references for orientation in our daily lives, each of our five senses triggers subtle subconscious changes in our minds, emotions, and bodies by means of biochemical and bioelectrical changes in brain and body chemistry. These changes literally affect the energy patterns of our bodies and, therefore, our relationship to the unseen world of potential that we are seeking to access. That is the essence of all "magical" practice.

Science tells us that everything is composed of atoms and atomic particles. These atoms are simply states of energy that combine themselves in various ways by means of their electrical charge. Because everything that makes up our bodies and the world that surrounds us is made of atoms endlessly combining in infinitely complex ways, ultimately, we are creatures of energy. By changing the energy pattern that defines us, we can change the pattern of the energies we draw to us. We can do this by using the four elements, because those four elements are also represented in the energies of the body. We unify these with our Spirit—our intention and will.

We relate to our world in four different but interrelated ways—mentally, emotionally, physically, and spiritually. These four functions are each manifested in an energy field that coincides roughly with the location of our physical body. Some people call these fields *auras*. Each field has an energy signature of its own and, taken together, they make up the energy signature that is uniquely yours. This is very much like a chord in music that is made up of several separate notes that, when taken together, make a single combined harmony. By using components such as scents, music, colors, and objects, we can act on these energy fields and make subtle changes in them. This allows us to change our alignment both in the physical world and our alignment with the energies of the Greater Universe that we wish to draw to us.

The Elements of Wishing

Once you have determined your goal and decided on the Moon time that is most appropriate to work on this objective, it is time to assemble a collection of physical objects that symbolize that objective and put them in a physical location where the work on your process can be focused. This is not just a collection of things that feel good or look theatrical. Although they should be pleasing to you and represent the essence of your goal, there is a larger purpose behind the selection. The purpose of the spell is the creation of a "mini-universe" that will be a specific focal point to concentrate the particular energy that you wish to bring into your life. It should contain a specific selection of things to make this area a generator of tuned energy. When you arrange a focal point for spell-work, assemble a collection of objects and elements that includes representatives from each of the elements chosen for their alignment with the purpose you have in mind, and for their ability to cause an alignment within you with that purpose.

But there is more to this assemblage than choosing things for their power or magical value. More than anything else, what attunes you to your connection with the magical, celestial, or Divine is neither objects nor words, it is your feelings about them, your connection with them, and your sense of how they connect with higher energies. As human beings, we express this through our sense of what is beautiful and harmonious. No other creature possesses humankind's sense of the aesthetic—our awareness of and instinct for what is beautiful. While other creatures may have many of the same emotions (love and compassion, for example), invent tools to use to carry out tasks, develop verbal and nonverbal communication on a reasonably sophisticated level, and have developed problem-solving skills based on this communication and the ability for collective action to contribute to a common purpose, no other species possesses our sense of the beautiful—that which is pleasing to the senses and Spirit. And certainly no other species connects this instinct with their connection to the higher harmonies that constitute our Universe. The greatest monuments dating from remote antiquity are not those dedicated to people or politics, but to the Divine energies that interact with our world. From the exquisite cave paintings at Alta Mira; the temples of ancient Egypt, Babylon, and India; the cathedrals of medieval France; and countless masterpieces of art and music throughout the millennia, it is this awareness of the connection of the beautiful with the celestial and Divine energy that makes us unique as a species. This is the very connection that the elements of wish magic seek to make. You address your inner connection with the Greater Universe through your inner sense of the beautiful, the wonderful, and the exceptional.

This is the mechanism by which you bypass the rational mind that insists that the physical Universe is all that exists and you must go along according to the limitations of its laws, and allows the dreaming mind to connect with your higher selves and greater powers to determine that the miraculous is your birthright and is always possible. Each individual has his or her own sense of what constitutes beauty, and it is not the purpose of this work to arbitrate what that may be. But your selection of objects, blending of oils, and choice of music should be based on this instinct, because this is the essential Spirit you are seeking to address. It is important to remember when selecting any of the parts of the process that you examine the way they make you *feel*, whether they have a feeling about them that is consistent with the purpose of your work, rather than being just an intellectually chosen object picked for its correspondence to a list of things to assemble. This emotion-based judgment is your indicator of whether an object, scent, or sound will work, and you should develop your attunement with this faculty as an important magical sensitivity. It is truly said that while the mind holds the senses of the body, the heart holds the senses of the Spirit.

The purpose of spell-work, or "wish" magic, is twofold. While you are intending to draw to yourself the object of your desire, whether that object is a state of mind, body, heart, or Spirit, you are also focusing your intention and will to bring yourself into alignment with that goal. The hoped-for result should be a meeting somewhere in the middle. You cannot draw a thing to you if you are not in alignment with it, because then you would have nowhere to "put" it within yourself or your world. So while you are reaching outward with your will and intention to draw this thing or condition to you, you must work on yourself as well, to create a receptive state of being with which to welcome it when it arrives. The elements in the spell help you align not only your mind and your inner focus, but your physical vibrations as well. It is an important principle to remember that nothing can exist or occur that goes against the laws of the Universe it occupies. Magic is not a way of going against nature. It is a way of moving yourself and events into harmony with the laws of this Universe—of manipulating things so that they will flow your way. Your work is the act of planting a seed of an ideal reality, and preparing the way for this seed to grow and expand into your life.

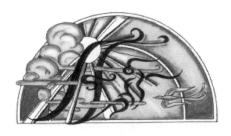 The dawn comes softly in colors of palest yellow and richest rose. As the Sun lifts from the horizon heralding a new day, warming the air with its radiance, a gentle breeze begins to stir, lifting the leaves on the trees and stirring the dew-wet grass. The new day brings a promise of new ideas and possibilities yet to be discovered. As the morning light increases, the breeze quickens. It tosses the treetops and ripples the grass into a sea of emerald light. Its energy tingles the senses and awakens the mind to curiosity. High in the sky, the clouds race before the wind until it becomes an unseen rushing torrent chasing old year's dead leaves, scouring the dust, penetrating every nook and crevasse with its insistent fingers. It pushes at your back, whipping your hair, clearing the cobwebs of the night's sleep away. Its thousand voices whisper, "Awake! Move! Live! This is a moment that has never been before, free to you for the shaping."

Air is the element of the mind, for it is with ideas that all things begin. It is no coincidence that the word *inspiration* comes from the Latin roots meaning "the act of breathing in." The first step in the creation of anything is the inspiration that begins to shape it. This is the moment of wonder and of exploring possibilities. Whether it concerns the form of an object or the content of a plan or project, everything begins with wondering "What if…?" or "Perhaps…," and then trying ideas on for size and testing their feasibility. So you begin any attunement work by addressing your relationship to its inspiration.

The element of Air represents the first appearance of pure Spirit and energy as it encounters the physical Universe on its way to physical manifestation. At this point, it is insubstantial, invisible. With Air, the pure impulse of spiritual energy becomes an idea or concept. Air is all about beginnings and ideas. All things must begin as a concept or archetype before they can become complete objects. From this conceptual stage, all things pass through the stages represented by the other elements before the final stage of concrete form—what we describe as "real."

Air is about Creation—the act of formulating an abstract concept and beginning its journey on the way to objective manifestation where it can take its place in the fabric of reality. Air is also about communication. Communication is an interaction between two points. This is a step away from the unity of pure energy. As an idea develops, it is as though a dialogue occurs between it and its creator to shape and test it before it enters the environment of action.

As important as Air is, it is, perhaps, the least noticed in our daily lives. We hardly notice ourselves surrounded and enveloped by it, but only a few moments of being deprived of it will point out its immediate necessity in a very real way. Not only is the very breath in our bodies essential for survival, but its weight and pressure actually keep our bodies together. Without it we would literally explode. Without an idea, no other act of Creation is possible—energy remains without an idea or concept to give it location and substance. So all magic begins with the element of Air to define what is yet to be.

The element of Air is represented by scent and your sense of smell. You can achieve its representation with the oil you have blended, and from that oil you carry the scent—the formative concept—throughout the process, ingraining it into your consciousness, bypassing your inner instinct of denial and limitation, rooting the thought into the fabric of your being so that it can take form and substance through your intention. From the basic oil, you make the incense that will cleanse and charge the air around you. You anoint the candles that will fill the space with colored light. You make bath salts that cleanse your body and energize your Spirit. You anoint the physical objects that you use for your focus. You even make special ink to write your wish or spell. The basic oil blend is your wish spell condensed into a bottle that can be with you throughout the day and night to carry the focus of your intention wherever you go.

Scent in the Atmosphere—Incense

For the purpose of your magical work, it will be necessary to find a way to release the scent into the air around you. There are several ways to do this, but the oldest and most time-honored way is through burning incense.

There is always some debate as to which objects represent which primal elements. It can be argued that because essential oils come in a liquid form, they can be considered to represent the Water element. The same is true of incense. Because it is only by lighting it that we generate its scented smoke, is it a creature of Air or Fire? The ancient alchemical philosophers tell us that in this Universe, no thing is perfectly and purely a substance of just one element, but some combination of all of them. That pure condition only exists in the realm of archetypes, that is, pure conceptions. The air we breathe has traces of water, and the clouds themselves are simply water vapor that at high altitudes turns to ice, which could be described as the element Earth for its solidity. The air contains dust particles that are certainly the province of Earth. The only logic behind the choice of association is to evaluate the principal function of the object or substance you are using. The function of essential oil is not its liquid nature but its fragrance. The chief attribute of incense is not the burning ember it requires but the smoke and scent that ember releases. We use candles, not for their solidity, but for their light and color, so we associate them with Fire. And so incense is attributed to the element of Air.

Every ancient civilization we have encountered discovered the many joys of scented smoke—from burning simple resins and herbal mixtures to complex formulations of incense. Even the word *perfume* comes from two Latin words: *per*, meaning "through," and *fumum*, meaning "smoke." Incense acts in a doubly powerful way because, not only does it address the sense of smell, it also acts directly with the body's energy field. Its smoke permeates the air surrounding us. When it does this, the charge of the atomic particles that make up the smoke bond with the energy field around our bodies and literally changes its charge. It also does this with the air in a room or other space, literally changing the charge of the area to correspond with the desired alignment of the work.

Another value of the smoke is that it directly interacts with the skin. The skin is the largest organ of the body. It is constantly breathing and circulating, absorbing and expelling substances in and out of the pores. We can observe this when we perspire, because the perspiration contains waste matter as well as trace minerals (such as salt) from our system. If too many of these minerals are lost through the perspiration along with the moisture, it is necessary to replenish them or we become ill. Incense takes advantage of this function by allowing the skin to absorb small amounts of what the smoke contains. These substances act homeopathically with the body's chemistry and contribute to the minute biochemical changes that, in turn, change the body's energy alignment.

There are basically two types of incense: noncombustible and combustible. Noncombustible incense will usually not burn by itself. It needs to be put on something else that is burning (charcoal block) that is already hot enough to cause it to smolder and release the smoke. Usually herbal mixtures do not require fine grinding, and you can simply crush the ingredients finely enough to mix them evenly and toss them together like a salad. They also generally produce a heavier, thicker smoke. Combustible incense contains a chemical such as saltpeter (potassium nitrate) added to the scented ingredients that will burn like a charcoal block when it is lit. It requires more preparation, but has the advantage of being more convenient to use, because it does not need the help of charcoal blocks and braziers.

A word of general advice on making your own incense: Burning herbs do not necessarily smell the same as when they are in their natural state. If you are making a blend with crushed herbs, try each of the ingredients first by putting a pinch on a burning charcoal block. The same holds true for oils. It is a good idea to test a small batch of your recipe before committing yourself to a large-scale production that might not produce suitable results.

General Preparation of Incense

Grind the dry ingredients separately to as fine a powder as possible. Then sift the powder to make sure there are no unground pieces that will end up in your final mixture. For small batches you can use a mortar and pestle. For larger amounts you can use a blender or coffee grinder. Be sure you clean the grinder thoroughly after each use so that the herbs do not cross-contaminate each other and so that if you are also using the blender or grinder for food preparation, you do not get incense herbs in your food. It is a good idea to purchase a special blender or grinder to keep solely for your incense preparation. When you have prepared all the herbs separately, mix the dry ingredients together, then, add the liquid to the resulting mixture. This forms a paste that you will use to make the incense. Use only glass or glazed ceramic mixing bowls. Metal can react with the mixture and contaminate it. Wooden bowls can absorb the chemical ingredients, and this can cause contamination of any other substance you put into them afterward. Hard plastic mixing spoons are also advisable for this same reason. You can also use Popsicle sticks or tongue depressors (available cheaply and in large quantities from your hobby store). Use a separate one for each batch and discard them when you are done.

Here is another helpful hint: If you are using resins such as frankincense or myrrh tears, they can easily gum up your equipment and be very difficult to pulverize. Put them in the freezer for 15 to 30 minutes and they will be much easier to grind.

Finely ground powder can lose its scent quickly. It is a good idea to add some **orris root** to the mixture, as this will act as a fixative for the volatile oils so that your incense will retain its scent much longer.

Once you have made any of these incense forms and they are completely dry, it is advisable to store them in closed glass containers or sealable plastic bags away from the light. This will allow them to retain their scent much longer than if they were kept out in the open.

Incense Pellets

A loose mixture does not need to be finely ground and can be as simple as an assembly of crushed dried herbs and small chunks of wood, bark, and resins tossed with a quantity of scented oil to soak in. But the heavier ingredients will settle to the bottom of the container, leaving you with a mixture that burns with an uneven scent. Powdering all the dried ingredients will allow a much more reliable mixture. The next step up from this assembly is making incense pellets or cakes. Because they are thoroughly mixed, this will guarantee that you will have a consistent scent mixture as the cake burns. They will need to be burned on a charcoal block because they have no ingredients to allow them to ignite on their own. To do this you will need to add a binding agent to the original mixture. Prepare the binding agent first and set it aside. Once you have powdered your original mixture and mixed the dry ingredients together, drizzle in the oils slowly until the entire preparation has a uniform consistency. Then add the binding agent until you have a doughy paste. Now you can form the dough into small balls (about the size of a marble). Put them in a jar and let them dry for two to three weeks.

Binding Agents

Gum tragacanth: Dissolve 2 teaspoons of tragacanth powder in 1/2 pint of warm water, adding a little at a time as you stir so that it will not develop lumps. You may use a baker's whisk for this. Keep stirring the mixture until you have a consistency like pasty glue (white glue or a little thinner). Put it in a jar and give it a good shake to help break up any lumps that may have formed. Keep the jar in a cool place (not the refrigerator) for three days, shaking it daily.

Gum arabic: Place a tablespoon of the powdered gum into a medium-sized bowl and add 8 ounces (1 cup) of warm water. Whisk it gently until the gum is totally dissolved. Let the dissolved gum absorb the water until you have a thick, gelatin-like paste. Cover the bowl with a wet cloth and set it aside for about two hours to thicken. You can adjust the consistency by adding more gum or water.

Incense Sticks

If you are using a mixture that consists entirely of blended oil, you may prefer the convenience of incense sticks. Making handmade incense sticks from scratch is a long procedure, as each stick is hand-dipped in the combustible preparation and the whole batch must dry for a while before you can use them. As a good alternative, you can buy nonscented sticks that are already coated with a combustible material. They are sometimes sold at fireworks stores or you can buy them in quantity from any store Website that sells incense-making supplies. These are called *punks*, or incense blanks.

Punk sticks are made from bamboo splints coated with wood dust that are held together with a binder, such as the ones discussed earlier. As they rub together during shipping, some of this dust will come loose. Before scenting the sticks, you will need to clean this off. Take a handful of the sticks and put them head down in a plastic or paper bag. Holding the bag around the tops of the sticks, tap and shake it to allow the loose dust to collect in the bottom. This will keep the dust from flying everywhere, and then you can neatly dispose of it.

Prepare a mixture of your scented oil in a carrier. Rubbing alcohol (Isopropyl alcohol) is a good choice for this unless you have access to DPG (dypropylene glycol). Some people recommend Everclear or cheap vodka for this, but they both contain small quantities of water that will cause your oil to bead on the surface and give you uneven coverage. Use about 1 ounce of oil to 1/4 ounce of carrier. If you are using a thick, resinous oil, such as frankincense or sandalwood, you will need to use more carrier—about 1/2 ounce carrier to 1 ounce of oil. You may want to experiment with the proportions here. You want a good, strong scent, but not one that is overpowering. Oils come in many different viscosities depending on the type and brand you prefer. You may need to do a little experimenting to determine what is best for you.

Pour about an ounce of your oil and carrier blend in a 9″ × 12″ × 3″ baking pan you have purchased especially for this task. Tilt the pan until the oil covers the bottom of the pan. Then lay about 25 sticks in the oil and gently roll them until the oil is absorbed.

Another convenient way to make sticks in large quantities is by dipping them. Use a tall, narrow glass container such as those used to store spaghetti pasta. If you cannot find one, or the ones you find are too tall, use the empty glass container from a seven-day candle. These are an ideal height for regular-length sticks. Clean the glass carefully with hot water and soap to remove all traces of wax and soot before you begin or this will ruin your incense sticks. Fill the glass container with the oil/carrier mixture and dip the bundles of punks. Allow the punks to remain in the mixture about five minutes to make sure they are thoroughly saturated. Again, this will take some experimentation. The quality of punk sticks can vary by manufacturer. Some coatings are denser than others. Try a few to get the timing right to be sure that you leave them in the solution long enough to get full saturation, but not so long that it will cause the coating to dissolve.

When the sticks are thoroughly saturated, spread them out on newspaper to dry. Bag them in sealable plastic bags or tightly closed gallon canning jars when they are slightly damp, but not totally dry. They keep well like this. Store any remaining oil/carrier solution in a jar to use later for more sticks.

Combustible Incense

Combustible incense is made of the finely ground herb and oil blend, as you have prepared for the incense sticks, mixed with saltpeter (potassium nitrate) to allow it to ignite, and charcoal to keep it burning. These ingredients are mixed with a binder to allow the incense to hold its shape such as the gum arabic and gun tragacanth mixtures described earlier.

Charcoal: Powdered charcoal is sold at church supply stores and some herbal specialty shops. Use pure powdered charcoal, as it has practically no smell. Do **not** use the charcoal sold for barbeque grills because it has other agents in it that will burn with an unpleasant smell that will spoil your incense. If you choose, you can grind up the self-igniting charcoal blocks sold for use in incense braziers. These already contain the saltpeter.

Your charcoal, saltpeter, herbs, and resins need to be ground to a fine powder. You can do this with a pestle and mortar. Do not put the charcoal in a blender because the dust will go everywhere. Use a ratio of roughly 14 parts of powdered charcoal to 6 parts of the other ingredients—in other words, to 14 parts of powdered charcoal, add 1/2 part of saltpeter, 3 parts of finely ground herbs, 1 part of powdered resin, and 1 1/2 parts of essential oil.

Mix the dry ingredients together. Add your essential oils a little at a time so that they are uniformly mixed throughout the mixture. Now add the saltpeter. You should put in 10 percent of the total weight of your mixture. **Measure this carefully.** If you add too much, the end product stinks as it burns and will ignite too quickly; too little, and it is difficult to keep lit. Add the binding agent slowly until you have made a thick paste. Form the paste into slender cones, roll it into "ropes" (like you did when you played with clay as a child) or round, flat disks. If you make them into chunky balls, they will be much more difficult to ignite. Dry them in a dark, airy place covered with a thin piece of gauze or cheesecloth to keep dust from settling on them. (They will get moldy if you do not allow the air to circulate around them freely.) When they are completely dry, store them in a cool, dry place.

Alternatives to Incense

Sometimes heavy smoke will trigger smoke alarms or provoke sneezing or asthma. There are also places where incense is not allowed. No matter how powerful or carefully chosen your scent, it will not be effective if the carrier for it makes the participants ill. Diffusers neatly bypass these problems. This is a shallow dish or bowl set on a stand above a votive candle or tea light. The dish is filled with water and a few drops of oil are added. As the candle warms the water, the scent is released into the air. This does not have the same powerful effect as incense, but is a viable alternate on occasions when incense smoke is not desirable.

You might also want to try a lightbulb ring. These are either metal or pottery rings that fit around the base of a lightbulb. They have a shallow groove running around them to hold a few drops of your scented oil. The heat of the lightbulb will heat up the ring that, in turn, warms the oil, releasing its scent. Metal ones are preferable to pottery ones because pottery rings are usually unglazed. The oil will permeate the pottery, and can be nearly impossible to remove if you wish to use the ring for a different scent. If you wish to use pottery, you will need a different ring for each scent. The advantage of the unglazed pottery here is that it is easily marked with a permanent marker so you can tell which ring you have used for which scent.

If neither a diffuser nor incense is workable in a situation, you can put a few drops of oil in a small spray bottle filled with a mixture of water and isopropyl (rubbing) alcohol or DPG (dypropylene glycol) and use it like any air freshener. The alcohol and water will evaporate quickly, leaving only the scent. This can also be sprayed directly onto the skin and clothing. If you do not wish to put the oil directly on your skin or clothes, you can put a few drops on a cotton ball or scrap of cloth and wear it in a bag around your neck. You can also put the oil on a small piece of cloth and use it like a dryer sheet in the laundry. This will allow the fragrance to permeate the fabric of your clothes and bedding without the risk of staining it.

The element of **Fire** represents passion and action. After an idea is conceived, it requires Fire to activate it and put it into motion or it will remain only a concept. Fire is the element that energizes and enlivens. This is the spark of life that puts things in motion.

Fire is also a primal need. We are told that it was humankind's mastery of fire that separated us from the animals and gave us the evolutionary edge to begin the long ascent up the ladder to civilization. Fire means protection, both in its capacity to dispel the shadows and drive away the darkness, and by warming us and making us more comfortable, which, in turn, makes us stronger and less likely to become ill. It lights our way and drives back predators, and in many ways, relieves stress mentally, emotionally, and physically. On another level,

Fire drives away the shadows of doubt, fear, and ignorance. It is the fire's heat at the forge that tempers metal, making it flexible and strong for tools and weapons. On a personal level, Fire is what tempers and tests us. The heart that has not been tested by the fires of life, passion, and adversity is the heart less strong and wise. Ideas not tested by analysis and opposition can remain unclear or faulty. Muscles and bodies, un-challenged, become soft and weak. Fire represents the transformative processes that translate potential into action.

When we do magic, Fire, represented by candles, is an integral part of the process. The candle's flame provides an energy all its own that puts vibrancy and life into all the other components. It can be said that the purest part of Fire is its light. When pure light encoun-ters a prism, it is broken into a rainbow of color called the *spectrum*. But the spectrum of energies is not limited to the color we see with our eyes. In the same way that light is broken into color by a prism, pure energy encountering physical manifestation is broken into a spec-trum of energies that range from those vibrations we can experience with our senses to many others that we cannot, all corresponding in vibration to the spectrum of color. All vibrations, whether color, sound, or physical energies, correspond to one another because, no matter how they are perceived, they can all be defined in the same way, that is, by a function of *frequency*, *wavelength*, and *amplitude*. This may sound very complex, but simply put, all forms of energy travel in a way that can be mapped in the form of a curvy line called a *sin* (pro-nounced "sign") *wave*. Wavelength tells us how wide each segment is, and amplitude tells us how tall. Frequency tells us how fast the line is moving. Regardless whether the energy is perceived as sound, color, or physical vibration, all energy can be placed on the spectrum. We have different senses that perceive different parts of it. Our eyes see the color part, and our ears hear the sound part. There are also large parts of it that we have no cognitive senses to register, but they are there just the same, and are affecting us whether we consciously reg-ister their presence or not.

The energies of our body and Spirit also correspond to these col-ors. Therefore, color makes a strong connection when we wish to attune ourselves to specific Universal Energies, because it is in a har-monic relationship to them. The vibration of Fire keys our awareness to them and connects us to them. Each color relates to a particular resonance of energy. By choosing the appropriate color candles and other elements of our magical working, we intensify the connection to the resonance of the purpose or goal. When colors are combined into a single, rolled beeswax taper or poured in layers into a glass, they combine their energies to form a single energy of focus.

The Energies of Color and Light

White (Pure Light, Completion, Focus, Expansion): Before light is dispersed into the separate colors of the rainbow by a prism, it begins as pure White, or clear light. White light contains the full spectrum of energies unified into one ray of single purpose, and represents all the energies of the spectrum concentrated into a single force. It is truly centered in itself and lacks nothing. It specifies nothing, but manifests as all in one. White represents intensity and expansive intent. If you cannot find the right color candle, White will often suffice as a substitute choice, especially in healing work, as it can represent the complete energy form of the body and Spirit. Stones associated with White are clear quartz, moonstone, and diamond.

Red (Mars, Energy, Passion, Intensity, Aggression): Red represents power in its most primitive form, manifested in the base chakra, where the primal Earth energy first enters the body at the base of the spine. Red energy is passionate and energetic. This can mean lust and anger, as well as passion, survival, and determination. And although it is dangerous in some aspects, without it there would be no survival on this physical plane. Red and Black combined in a candle will give you the energy of Red's protection and defense along with Black's purification and shielding. Stones associated with Red are garnet, ruby, and red agate. Its musical tone is the key of G#.

Rose (Venus, Pleasure, Love, Expansion): Rose is an aspect of the Red energy that also coincides with the base chakra, but resonates with the heart center as well. Rose represents passion on the physical plane and love on the spiritual and emotional plane. This is the love that bonds us together and flows from the mother to nurture and nourish the child, as well as the tie that draws lovers and passion. While Red is about physical passion, Rose is about emotional intensity and well-being. Rose is the energy that enables the individual not just to survive but to grow and flourish. Stones associated with Rose are pink tourmaline and rose quartz.

Orange (Sun, Assertive, Encouraging, Courage, Identity, Confidence): Orange banishes the darkness like the light of the Sun. This is the energy of hearth and home, the love of the young, and the safety of the dwelling. It is the ray of true courage that defends the just cause. It is also the ray of self-awareness and pride in personal achievement. Orange encourages creativity, independence, and self-esteem. Use Orange candles when you are interviewing for a job in order to increase your confidence. You can also use them to deal with fears and phobias, such as fear of storms or of the dark. Stones associated with Orange are carnelian, pad parajah, zincite, and citrine. Its musical tone is the key of A#.

Yellow (Mercury, Sun, Joy, Mental Clarity, Agility): Yellow is the color of sunshine and joy—the heart of dancing and song. The yellow ray is the power of hope expressed as the *power of mind*. Yellow assists in manifesting change because it encourages brightness and cleverness—the joy of the Spirit in all things that are new and unique. This is curiosity in the most positive sense, indicating all the capacities of the mind and Spirit that see the world as new and fresh. Yellow encourages mental clarity and personal flexibility. Stones associated with Yellow are topaz and heliodor. Its musical tone is the key of C.

Green (Venus, Healing, Prosperity, Growth): Green is the color of regeneration, restoration, and renewal on both the spiritual and physical levels. It is referred to as the color of the heart because the heart is the metaphor for the ever-springing force of love and renewal. This is the ray of the Mother and of Mother Earth, for it represents the renewing bounty of the physical world. This is the ray of selfless nurturing and creativity without possessiveness. As such, it is the color of artists and gardeners, because they participate in the ongoing unfolding of the beauty of the world while releasing their works to become parts of the sum total of its richness. In a more worldly sense, green is used as the color of money and prosperity magic, as well as for healing and convalescence.

Green and Rose together make a powerful combination both for inviting love into one's life and for healing and renewal. Stones associated with Green are emerald, jade, and green aventurine. Its musical tone is the key of D.

Turquoise: The color Turquoise promotes heart/mind balance to better achieve the Soul's purpose of "right expression"; it helps lift depression or negativity, and through deeper harmony helps better utilize the forces of nature. It ties together the Green light of the loving and compassionate heart with the will and communication associated with the throat. This helps to stimulate clairvoyance and psychic abilities. It is associated with the rarely discussed eighth chakra located in the thymus (located near your left armpit, midway between your throat and your heart), which is associated with the Soul's evolution. Use Turquoise candles in work involving psychic awareness and attunement to the Higher Self. It is also used in work concerning one's spiritual destiny and purpose. Stones associated with Turquoise are turquoise, aquamarine, hemimorphite, and chrysocholla. Its musical tone is the key of D#.

Blue (Moon, Will, Communication, Expression): Blue expresses will and intention, the clear focused force of perception and expression. Blue helps in bringing down the barriers to self-awareness by bringing the nature of these barriers into true perspective. In doing so, Blue is also a teacher, allowing you to bring your insight to bear on obstacles that may be hindering your life. It opens inner channels, focusing and refining the energies, allowing conscious awareness of the higher vibrations. Stones associated with Blue are blue sapphire and blue topaz. Its musical tone is the key of E.

Violet (**Indigo**) (Saturn, Inner Wisdom, Guidance): Violet is the energy that promotes understanding those matters that extend from and deal with the Higher Self and its relation to the Greater Universe. This is the path by which the voice of the inner self reaches the conscious self. Violet energy's center is the brow. It is also connected to the Higher Consciousness energy of this Universe and can be a great guide to wisdom of many kinds. Violet is a powerful path to healing because it reveals the higher nature of the causes of many situations and conditions. Use Violet candles when working with spirituality and inner peace, or when asking for wisdom to deal with a difficult problem, because they help with relaxation and meditation. Stones associated with Violet/Indigo are lapis lazuli and amethyst. Its musical tone is the key of F#.

Purple (Jupiter, Majesty, Abundance, Higher Awareness): Purple (royal red violet) is the color of power and balance because it is the perfectly balanced union of Red, the primal animal drive, and Blue, the pure expression of evolved higher will. The Purple ray centers at the crown of the head and is sometimes referred to as the Crown Lotus of Awareness. This is the color of the true ruler and monarch and is sometimes ascribed to the crown chakra rather than Clear or White because it holds the understanding of the complete nature of the human being, and from this understanding come both discipline and compassion. Purple and Violet candles are good to use when working for psychic development. Stones associated with Purple are amethyst and purple tourmaline. Its musical tone is the key of G.

Black (Contraction, Protective, Purging, Banishing, Grounding): Black draws all rays of energy into itself but emits nothing. It balances and levels all vibrations and acts as a natural grounding element. It is the perfect mask, for it has no reflection and reveals nothing except its existence. Black absorbs all colors and emits none. This makes it an excellent choice for protecting and purifying. It draws the specified energies into itself and disposes of them. Black candles are sometimes referred to as reversing candles. Stones associated with Black are onyx and black tourmaline.

Brown (Grounding, Practicality): In matters concerning commercial property and legal matters, brown makes a good choice. It is the color of the earth, indicating solidity and firmness. Brown candles are often used in work involving the sale of real estate or other significant property, such as furniture or vehicles. This is also the color candle to choose if you are seeking to return lost objects. The stone associated with Brown is Tiger's-eye.

Safety With Candles

Ideally, once your candles are lit for your work, unless the spell specifies otherwise, do not extinguish them yourself. Allow them to burn out completely. When using anything flammable in a ritual (or in the rest of your life), you must have respect for its potential to damage or destroy things. NEVER leave a burning candle alone with children! Be aware that, if you have pets, the candles and other ritual items should be placed so that they will not be able to accidentally interfere with them. If you wish to leave your candles burning for several days, take great care to place them so they will not be disturbed and where they will be away from an open window where the curtains might blow across them. If you have put them on a shelf, make sure that the shelf above them is far enough away so that it does not char or catch fire from the heat of the flame beneath it. If you need to leave the candles burning, you may also place the entire setup on a metal tray or on a stone fireplace hearth or mantle, making sure that the candles will not fall over against a flammable surface.

Preparing and Charging Your Candles

Preparing a candle for use in magical work is called "dressing" it. This is the process of cleaning it, and then anointing it with your oil formula. As you do this, you will charge it with the thought and energy of your intention. You may do this as a part of the preparation for the spell or as a part of the ritual itself.

1. Wash the candles with warm soapy water to remove any grease or dust. Then rinse them in salt water to purify them.

2. Inscribe the essence of your purpose for that candle into the wax using a pencil, ballpoint pen, or any other easily held instrument that will scratch the surface.

3. Anoint them with the appropriate oil. Put a drop of the oil on your finger, then, starting at the middle of the candle, rub the oil outward toward the ends until the candle is entirely lightly coated with the oil. As you do this you should be centered and focused, holding the purpose of your work clearly in mind. Wrap it carefully in plastic wrap or put it in a refrigerator box where it will remain clean until you use it.

The Shape of Your Candles

Candles come in a wide variety of shapes and sizes. Tapers are long and thin and may vary in length from about 3 inches to as long as 16 inches. Their length determines how long they will burn. They are made out of wax, which can be composed of paraffin, tallow (animal fat), beeswax, or some combination of these ingredients. Their composition determines how hot they will burn, how long, and how much they will drip. Some candles are dripless, that is, they are made of wax that will be consumed completely as it burns. Others drip in varying degrees. Be sure that no matter what the label says or what they are made of, the holder you place them in has a wide enough saucer underneath it in case they drip.

Votive candles are small and chubby and are about 2 inches high. They should be burned in a glass or metal holder because they are made so that their wax liquefies and is consumed slowly by the fire. Also, their wick is usually held in place by a small square of metal. As the candle burns down, the wick holder can heat up, and has the potential to crack the votive holder. It is a good idea to place the votive cup on a dish or saucer in case the heat of the candle causes the glass to crack and break. This will also protect the surface the holder is sitting on so that it will not be damaged by the generated heat. The wax liquefies quickly after it is lit, and the candle will burn for several hours. Use them in work that will only take you one sitting. Tea lights can be used in the same way as votives

Pillar candles are large and wide and will often burn for several days. Some will burn completely; others will drip and run from the sides. Make sure that there is an adequate dish under them to catch the drips and to avoid any fire hazard when they burn to the bottom. It is not a good idea to put them in a glass container that prevents dripping. They are not formulated to burn in this way, and the pool of wax can smother the wick, putting out the flame.

There is also a wide variety of single and multicolored container candles available. You can find them in glass and ceramic containers in a variety of shapes and sizes, including artistic-looking apothecary jars. Some are pre-scented; others are not. The size of the candle determines how long it will burn—small short ones will only burn for about a day; taller ones will burn longer. The tall cylindrical ones will burn for six to seven days. Sometimes you will be able to purchase the glass separately from the candle insert. In this case, it is a simple matter to prepare the candle as you would a taper or pillar and then slide it into the glass. Other container candles are poured into the container and have no vertical surface on which to put the oil. In this case, add a few drops of your oil blend as the candle burns. You can write your wish or purpose in the top of the wax of container candles instead of down the sides as you would a freestanding one.

A word of caution: Always place your candles on a fireproof surface. A small saucer, metal dish, or flat stone will do. Even though the candle is completely contained, the glass container can crack or break when the burning wick reaches the bottom to consume the last of the wax, because, like a votive, their wick is held in place with a metal square. Also, as the flame reaches the bottom, the glass can become hot and mar the surface where you have placed it.

Any candle spell can be done with votives or with tapers of varying length, depending on how long you want them to last. In addition, there are other candles available that have different shapes that can contribute to the intent and focus of your spell-work. Make your choice according to the meaning of the shape and the color most suited to the focus of your work. The following are some popular shapes, but there are many more available at candle and novelty shops. Dress and inscribe a shaped candle just as you would a plain one.

Cat or **Snake:** Cats and snakes are fluid, graceful creatures. Use these shapes for aligning with grace, subtlety, or stealth. Any animal shape can be used for requesting the aid of a Spirit helper or familiar. Snakes also help with transformation and change because of their ability to shed their old skin as they grow.

Dragon: Dragons connect us with ancient wisdom as well as power for protection. They make worthy advisors.

Male or **Female:** These are used for both love-drawing and healing. Write your name and birthday into the wax. As the candle burns, envision the barriers between you and the object of your desires melting with the wax. If you are using it for healing, write the name and birthday of the person you are healing into the wax. Mark horizontally down the back so there are seven equally spaced sections. Burn the candle each day for a week for the duration of each section while you meditate on the person, seeing them completely healed and strong in the light of the flame. Envision the flame carrying away any trace of injury or disease, leaving a clean and healthy body and Spirit.

Owl: Owls hunt at the time between day and night; therefore, they are known as the messengers between the worlds. They are silent hunters. Use an owl image for wisdom and insight to reveal the truth and find clarity on complex situations where the information may be confused or hidden.

Seven Knot: Write your wish into the wax, then burn one knot per day for seven days.

Skull: Use a skull candle when seeking wisdom and guidance from your ancestors or other plane guides. They also help when you are seeking to develop psychic gifts or other plane awareness, and for when you are working to heal mental and emotional disturbances.

Lamp of the Ancients

This is an interesting way to invoke the spirits of the ancient ancestors. For thousands of years, people did not use candles. Instead, they used lamps filled with animal or vegetable oil with a fiber wick. Although countless examples of these lamps can be seen in museums the world over, few people have ever seen one lit or know how simple they are to use. Some of them are more elaborate than others, but they all work on the same principle: a deep dish, shallow bowl, or container has a twist of fiber laying from the oil pool to the edge of the dish that allows the wick to draw oil into itself. Olive oil works beautifully for this. For the wick, use a cotton ball, a twist of sheep's wool, or length of heavy cotton cord. Take the cotton ball or wool and stretch and twist it until you have a fat, stubby wick, soak it in the oil, and lay it in the bowl with enough sticking out of the oil to light and remain on the side without falling in. The ancients made their lamp bowls with a slight depression on the side to hold the wick. The burning time depends on the length of the wick and quantity of the oil that is used.

Tapers From Beeswax Sheets

A satisfying way to make special candles without going to elaborate measures is to use beeswax sheets. These are formed sheets with a honeycomb pattern about 8″ × 16″ that come in a delightful variety of colors. They are convenient to use because beeswax sheets work easily at room temperature (70–80 °F). Use a standard prepared waxed 1/0 wick that you can get at hobby stores. Decide on the height of your candle and cut the sheet of wax accordingly. If you want more than one color, cut both sheets to the same size. To cut the wax, lay it flat on a nonstick surface, such as newspaper, and then use a pizza wheel that you have carefully cleaned with hot water and soap, and then wiped down with alcohol or acetone. It is important that the cutter be absolutely clean, because otherwise it can stick and drag in the wax.

Once you have the piece cut, lay it out on a clean surface and apply the oil blend to what will be the inner surface of the wax. You may even sprinkle it lightly with powdered herbs if you like. If you use any coarsely crushed herbs, they will pop and catch fire as the candle burns, so this is **not** recommended. Lay both sheets together if you are using more than one, and press one edge firmly together so that they form a bond. Then press the wick firmly into the flat spot. If the wax is not firmly seated around the wick, the candle will burn unevenly or not at all. Form the first wrap of wax firmly around the wick. Then roll the wax loosely around the rest using as little pressure as possible so you will not spoil the honeycomb pattern in the sheet. When the cylinder is rolled, wrap it gently in plastic wrap or waxed paper and place the candle in the refrigerator until you are ready to use.

All life on our planet evolved from the primordial ocean. Even millions of years from the first spark of life in a single-celled organism, our bodies are still mostly comprised of seawater and, without daily replenishment of moisture, we would quickly die. The air we breathe is full of microscopic moisture and, without this, our lungs would dry out and be unable to process oxygen into our bloodstream. In magical working, **Water** symbolizes the emotions. These are the primal driving impulses that direct our actions even before our thinking minds take over to analyze a situation. Addressing the Water element means dealing with our instincts. It is also about our ability to move with the flow of subtle energies that manifest as circumstances and events in our lives. The fluid nature of water gives it the power to find its way around obstacles in its path, and simply by this action, eventually wear them away. Water nourishes all life. Without it our green and blue planet would be nothing but a gray and desolate moonscape. Without feelings and emotions, our inner landscape is desolate. In a situation, our emotions dictate our ability to flow with the course of events and nourish our ability to relate and grow. Water is a powerful tool that we can use to reach our purpose or goal. We can use this emotional element to circumvent, wear away, or sweep away the obstacles from our path, whether they are external blockages or inner psychological limitations. We can also use this element to nourish and nurture our surroundings and our inner lives. This makes Water an important part of any magical working. One of the most powerful ways to incorporate this into your work is to take a magical bath.

Bath salts and oils work to change the vibration of your energy in much the same way that incense does. Bathing allows the oil to come into direct contact with the skin and adjusts the body's energy field by interacting with it in two ways. The chemical/atomic structure of the oil bonds with the energy field's free electrons to change its charge, and, therefore, its vibration. The oil permeates the skin to act homeopathically on both the body and brain chemistry to change your vibration internally. The scent that is breathed in along with the steam carries microscopic elements further into the bloodstream through the lungs and breathing passages, while the aromatherapy properties act on the brain to adjust the attunement of your body chemistry even further.

When taking a magical bath, it is important to remember to submerge your whole body, wetting your hair thoroughly along with the rest of you to get the full effect. Once you are completely wet, the warmth of the bath water opens the pores of the skin and relaxes the muscles, allowing you to slide into a meditative state more easily. This is an excellent time to listen to music that will enhance your mood and do some quiet meditation on your purpose. Allow an image of your goal to fill your mind until it feels as though you can touch it, smell it, experience it. Know that it is real. Take this time to enhance your belief and confidence that your goal is already fulfilled and manifesting. When you feel confident with this image, get out of the bath and gently pat yourself dry. Rubbing with a towel will remove too much of the oil, and your purpose at this point is to carry the scent and charge through the entire cycle of the process. If you are using candles that are intended to burn longer than one day, you may repeat the bath daily until the candles are done, using this time to meditate and reinforce your intention.

You may also use crushed herbs in your bath salts mixture. A handful of herbs makes a natural infusion of their essential properties, rather like making a giant cup of tea. If you choose to do this, however, do not just toss a handful of crushed herbs into the water. It may be lovely while you are bathing, but the resulting mess will hardly be worth the length of time it will take to clean it out of the tub. Put the herbs in a muslin bag that is sewn shut or an extra-large tea ball. This will allow them to infuse the bath water while keeping them contained, and save a lot of trouble with clean-up and clogged drains.

Bath magic can be a powerful tool when you are initiating change, transformation, or transition in your life. The act of removing your old clothes, washing away the old circumstances, and rising from the bath water, charged with all the new energies you wish to bring into your life can be powerfully symbolic as well as magically potent. As a part of this process, be sure you have new, clean clothes to put on when you are done. On many levels, this will signal that the new phase of your life has begun.

Oils and Your Skin

Essential oils are highly concentrated and may irritate the skin, especially in delicate, sensitive areas. Be sure that you check out your personal sensitivity before using them on your skin. Oils that may smell good and be magically tuned to your purpose—such as cinnamon, wintergreen, peppermint, and pennyroyal—can burn your skin if they are used in concentrated form. You may also have specific allergies that you may not be aware of until you test them. Some oils, such as pennyroyal, may be toxic in large quantities. Always do a preliminary test on a small patch of skin, such as the inside of your elbow, before using them in the bath. Also remember that mixing oils changes their chemical properties. Besides testing each one separately, test the mixture in its final combined form. Elements that may be harmless by themselves may react differently once you have mixed them. It is definitely not to your magical purpose to have a bath that burns or later causes a rash to break out while you are trying to meditate peacefully on your goal.

Bath Salts

The salt content in bath salts is the active ingredient that interacts with the energy fields of your body and initializes the change in its charge. You may choose from either sea salt or Epsom salts, or use a combination of the two. Sea salt is sodium chloride (NaCl) and different in chemical composition from Epsom salts, which is magnesium sulfate ($MgSO_4$). Consequently, they work in different ways with the energy fields of your body. It is important to use sea salt rather than regular table salt because the trace minerals found in it are energizing and add to the effect. Also, soaking in Epsom salts is helpful in drawing toxins from the body.

Bath salts are easy to make from ingredients found on most supermarket and pharmacy shelves. The base mixture can be mixed ahead of time in larger quantities and kept in a sealed container for an almost unlimited time. When you want a special blend, it is just one short step to making a small quantity for a special purpose by adding a few drops of the essential oil you have blended to suit your purpose, so that they will be directly tuned to the purpose you have in mind. This base mixture is also ideal for making any scented salts for relaxation, beautification, and the general pleasure of taking a luxuriously scented bath. You can use any blend of essential oils from the ones you prepare yourself to ones that are available commercially.

Base Mixture

Mix the following salts together thoroughly in a large bowl using your hands or a large wooden spoon reserved just for this purpose:

- 4 cups Epsom salts.
- 2 cups sea salt.
- 1/2 cup cornstarch or powdered milk.
- 1 tsp. essential oil.
- 8 drops vegetable food coloring (if desired).

After you have thoroughly mixed the base elements, you may want to add food coloring to your mixture one drop at a time, mixing it in well until the mixture is the color that you desire. You can make different batches of colored base and add them together to make multicolored salts. If you want a mixture that is a compound color, that is, purple (red + blue), orange (red + yellow), or green (yellow + blue), prepare the color in a separate dish, mixing the two primary colors together until you have the shade you want. Then use this to add to the salts base. Each batch of colored salts should be stored in its own separate watertight container until you are ready to use it.

Once the base mixtures are prepared, you can add the scent to as little or as much of them as you need. Using the oil blend you have previously prepared, add it in to the base drop by drop, working it thoroughly with your hands until your sense of smell tells you that the smell is strong enough. Use 1 cup for each bath. Be sure to work the mixture thoroughly to make sure there are no clumps in the salt and that all of the mixture is completely permeated. When it is thoroughly mixed, spread it all out on waxed paper until it dries. Store it in a closed container so that the scent will not dissipate.

A note about food coloring: Colored bath mixtures are fun to have and make a good way of telling one from another, **however**, a little color goes a long way. If you use too much color in the product, it will color your skin and stain your tub when you use it. Vegetable food coloring is a little more expensive but is less likely to tint your skin and hair. Whichever one you choose, use it sparingly.

Bath Balls and Bombs

If you find that the salt content of bath salts is not desirable, you can use bath bombs instead. The effect will not be as intense, but the aromatherapeutic and oil properties will be just as strong. This is also a good way to prepackage your scent that adds a little bit of fun to the experience. Here are recipes for two different kinds that are easy to make in your kitchen.

Fizzing Bath Bombs

For equipment you will need:
- 1 medium-sized glass mixing bowl.
- 1 half-cup measuring cup or other small bowl, such as a custard cup.
- Tin or plastic mold to shape the mixture, such as ones used for candy, soaps, larger butter shapes, or a plastic ice tray that makes shallow dome-shaped or novelty ice cubes—these should be slightly flexible to help ease the finished product out of the forms.

   🐚 A pair of rubber gloves.

The ingredients are:

   🐚 1 1/2 cups bicarbonate of soda (baking soda).

   🐚 1/2 cup citric acid (this looks like powdered sugar and can be found in the grocery store with the canning supplies).

   🐚 6 drops of essential oil.

   🐚 8 to 12 drops of food coloring (if desired).

   🐚 1/2 teaspoon sweet almond oil (available at health food stores) or mineral oil (I prefer almond oil because it is better for the skin). Put 1/2 teaspoon into the mixture and grease the inside surface of the molds so that the little cakes will not stick when you turn them out after drying.

Step 1: Coat the insides of the molds with the sweet almond oil and set them aside.

Step 2: Combine the bicarbonate of soda and the citric acid in the glass bowl, making sure they are thoroughly mixed.

Step 3: In the 1/2-cup measuring cup or custard cup, put 6 drops of essential oil (if you prefer a stronger scent, you may use a few more drops of oil), 1/2 teaspoon sweet almond oil, and 8 to 12 drops food coloring. Pour this mixture a little at a time into the dry ingredients, stirring quickly so that they will not start fizzing.

Step 4: Wearing the rubber gloves, work the ingredients together completely until the mixture starts to stick together like cookie dough.

Step 5: Press the mixture into the molds firmly so that any air bubbles left in it from mixing are forced out of it. The firmer you pack them now, the less likely they will crumble when you turn them out after drying.

Step 6: Allow the molds to dry for 24 to 36 hours (until they are powdery to the touch). Turn the molds over and flex them gently or tap them with a wooden spoon to loosen and dislodge the pieces.

Step 7: Pack the bath bombs in an airtight container or tightly sealed zipper-lock bag so that the moisture in the air will not spoil them.

Bath Oil Balls

This recipe calls for the same equipment as the Fizzing Bath Bombs. The ingredients are:

- 1/4 cup powdered milk.
- 3 Tbsp. cornstarch.
- 3 Tbsp. borax powder.
- 2 1/2 Tbsp. distilled water or witch hazel.
- Vegetable food coloring (if desired).
- 1 tsp. mineral or almond oil.
- 1 1/2 tsp. essential oil.

Combine the dry ingredients (powdered milk, borax, and cornstarch) in the mixing bowl until they are thoroughly mixed. Combine the distilled water and food coloring in the small cup. Slowly add this to the dry ingredients, stirring as you go. Now gently drizzle the almond oil and essential oil over the mixture. Wearing rubber gloves, use your hands to combine all the ingredients, working the mixture until it is the consistency of cookie dough and it is thoroughly mixed. Using about a teaspoon of dough for each, roll the mixture into small balls and set out on wax paper. This will make about 10 balls. Let dry for 24 to 36 hours. Store the balls in an airtight container until you are ready to use them.

Showers

Sometimes a bathtub is not available, or, if it is, taking a long bath is not feasible (such as in a dormitory or other communal living situation). If this is the case, you can do this process in a shower. After wetting your body thoroughly, scrub with a handful of coarse sea salt, kosher salt, or Epson salts. Once this is done, take a clean washcloth and put some of the magical oil on it that you have diluted in a light oil base. A good base oil for this is either jojoba oil, grape seed oil, or almond oil because they have no discernable scent of their own. Use about 1/4 cup of oil base for a few drops of essential oil blend. Put some of this on a washcloth intended only for this purpose (this is because the oil base will stain the washcloth and both the scent and oil mark will be difficult to remove), and rub yourself down with it. This allows the oil to permeate your pores that have been opened by the warm shower, and the aromatherapy can do its work while you complete your meditation in a more private place.

Mists

Another way to permeate your skin with the scent is to prepare an atomizer or sprayer with which you can mist the fragrance all over.

You can disperse the essential oil into rubbing alcohol and then dilute this with distilled water. A few drops to 1/4 cup of carrier liquid should be enough. If you try this and the smell is not strong enough, you may add a few more drops of oil. You can test it on your inner wrist to make sure it is right before using it. After you spray, wait for the alcohol in the mixture to evaporate before making your final decision.

If you do not wish to use a carrier for your preparation, there is an even easier way to compose a spray that does not involve essential oils at all. Use the herbs that the oils are taken from and brew them into a strong tea. When it is cool, strain out the herbs, and then dilute the resulting liquid by one half with water. This can easily be used to mist yourself or an area with a delightful light fragrance. Although the scent will not last as long as an essential oil, it will infuse the area with the magical property of the herbs and trigger the aromatherapy response desired. If you wish to keep this preparation for a long time, add a few drops of alcohol to the mixture to prevent it from going bad.

Once you have the idea of Air, the energy of Fire, and the emotion of Water, **Earth** represents manifestation in its final form. Earth is the ground under our feet, the solidity of all things. It is all essence of archetypes and concepts translated into physical form. The fragile concept represented by Air has now come full circle into the realm of the concrete and tangible. The element of Earth represents abundance in our lives, because here we see the fruits of our labors. All your efforts to shape energy come to fruition here as a result of aligning yourself through the other elements. This is the result of the change working within yourself and your life—enhanced awareness, greater knowledge or personal strength, and the resulting release from the inhibiting and limiting factors that have controlled your life in this issue. Consequently, what you choose to represent the Earth element in your process should be a concrete object that embodies what you wish to achieve.

As you choose an image to embody the purpose of your wish, you are doing what people have done in countless ways over the millennia to connect with Universal Energy. Each age and civilization has found its own particular means of physically expressing the connection with the Infinite. In the early ages of humankind, it was almost universally believed that art was the means of communication with the universal spectrum of energies. An image of a person, animal, or object was created in order to draw upon its energy or power. The concept of art existing for its own sake did not become popular until relatively recently in human history. Paintings and sculpture have great power to move us deeply on many levels. By incorporating form, color, and content, works of art strike chords on an almost instinctual level, moving us through our emotional levels and deeper to the source of those emotions. This bypasses reason and the opportunity for the rational mind to deny or reject the energies and feelings that these powerful images stir within us. These images free us from the civilized obligation to analyze and censor, allowing the inner self to respond. It is at this inner level that change and empowerment can take root and grow. We can only do so much with our conscious mind. If change were a conscious, rational process, you would have taken steps to make those changes already. You are working to reach into your deeper levels, to the wellsprings from which your life and character come, and find the connections with the archetypal forces that exist in you.

If your work concerns a person, place, or object, you should have a picture or representation of that individual, place, or thing. If your goal is less concrete—such as *happiness* or *relaxation*, for example— try to find a picture or object that captures the feeling you imagine your goal would feel to you if you had achieved it. It must arouse a personal, emotional response in you, as well as a mental one of recognition. For instance, if you are working for an increase in income, simply putting a pile of coins or a picture of money in place would not be sufficient unless you have some emotional tie to physical money. Instead, find a representation of what this abundance would feel like and the things and emotional state you could achieve by having it. If you are seeking employment, find a representation of people doing the kind of work you want to do as well as examples of their product. You are using this representation as an emotional trigger to stimulate these vibrations within yourself. This is the focal point of your spell-work—the object that will be the focus of manifestation of the energies you want. It is important to have this focus as direct and specific as possible.

Ideas and concepts are not always easy to pin down of a single image, so sometimes people use tarot cards to represent them. Tarot cards come in an almost endless variety of artistic styles, and it is the nature of the deck that there are cards representing virtually every emotion, state, and human condition. When you have chosen the card that best describes your goal, create a photocopy enlargement of it to use in your final spell. This will ensure that your deck remains intact while giving you a prominent focal point for your spell.

If you wish, you can use a three-dimensional object such as a statue or model toy to represent this focal point. Appropriately shaped candles are an excellent choice because they have the added essence that they can be dressed with your oil blend, inscribed with your declaration of intention, and burned to release their energy.

Using a Crystal as a Focal Point

For spells of a less concrete nature, such as aligning with a quality of essence, you may use a crystal. Charge the crystal with the intention that it forms a gateway to the qualities you wish to enhance. By meditating with it, you can put the feelings and intentions you have about the issue into it. This can be highly effective in the case of long-term self-development work. If you are working with crystals, you should carry the stone you have chosen around with you in your pocket or a bag around your neck—any method that keeps it in contact with you at all times—for at least several days before the time of your spell-work. By doing this, it will become charged with your vibration pattern.

The crystal or stone you use for this should be a new one that you have not used for anything before and will not use for anything again after. A crystal has a signature vibration pattern just like a person or any life form does. This is determined by the type of crystal it is. Crystals are made by stacking the molecular structure in a very regular and predictable way. Each of the elements in its structure has a very specific vibration pattern that is unique to that element. When a mild electrical charge passes through the crystal, it oscillates (vibrates) in a very particular way. The vibration is unique to that crystal and does not change. Its charge, which is like its memory (the record of its experiences, programming, and activity, and the forces that have been exerted on it) is held in its surface in the degree and pattern of ionic bonding of the atomic structure, and it is this surface charge that you are going to clear and bring into alignment with you. In its long history since its formation, it has been subjected to many random natural stimuli—intense cold, heat, pressure, and electromagnetic and gravitational forces—and its behavior will have been affected to some degree by all of them. You do not want the stone's work to be muddled by old accidental patterns that you did not intend to be there. So the first step in working with your crystal is to clear it. By clearing the crystal, you realign the surface ionization in preparation for charging your stone with its particular purpose or message. This is similar to formatting a computer disc prior to storing information on it. Not only is the surface cleaned of old unwanted information, but it is organized in such a way that it is now compatible with the way in which the computer will store and use the information to be placed in it.

There are many methods for clearing. "Salt clearing" requires submerging the crystal in salt water (often sea salt is specified) for some period of time. This method is not generally recommended because it will completely remove all surface ionization from your stone, removing every bit of personality or purpose from the stone by wiping it blank. In all but the most unusual cases, this process is extreme and excessive.

If you wish to use a passive method of clearing, leave your crystal on a sunny windowsill in a quiet room for a week. This will allow some of the random charge to dissipate. You may also use running water. Just let the cool water from your faucet rinse the stone. This does not always work very well with heavily chlorinated and fluoridated city water, but water that has not been extensively treated usually will work just fine. This reduces the surface ionization while leaving its character intact. A variant of this is to take a bath or shower while wearing your stone.

The most effective method to clear a crystal prior to working with it, is called *"impulse cleansing."* This is very much like going to a pet store to find a puppy or kitten. There may be many there that are wonderfully cute and fuzzy, but when you pick up that special one, your eyes meet, your hearts touch, and something inside you says, "Mine." It is like wrapping your heart around it with one surge of energy through your hands—you "love" at it. By doing that with a crystal, you clear the stone and align it with your personal energy pattern. Find a quiet place to relax a moment with your stone, and hold it gently between the palms of both hands. Take a deep breath, and, as you exhale the breath, allow any tension you may be feeling to leave your body. As your body relaxes, your mind also relaxes, becoming clearer and more focused. Now, look into your stone and envision it filled and engulfed in a pure white dazzling light that drives out everything else. Picture in your mind pouring this brilliant light into the stone with one pure focus of your will and heart put into one burst of thought such as, "Mine!" "Clear!" "Clean!" or whatever feels appropriate. This will establish a clear connection between your energy field and that of your crystal. The next step is to charge or program it to your specific purpose.

Charging the stone is done in the same way. Once you have relaxed and cleared your mind, consider what you would like to have your crystal help you do. Remember to keep it clear and simple. Then, when you are sure you have it just right, you set it into the crystal with the same sort of impulse you used when you cleared it—one straight surge from your heart through your hand. You may think or even say aloud, "Yes!" or "Do it!" However you phrase it, the actual programming is done with that one strong surge.

As you progress with the work, when you have a chance—at least twice a day, morning and evening—you should take it out, oil it with the oil of your purpose, and tell it what you want it to do, and who or what it represents. Work with the crystal between your hands to infuse it with the vibration of your emotions and your goals. After a few days, it will take on the pattern of the object you want. Use it as a point of focus during the spell-work just as you would a picture or statue. Be sure that you relate to it on all levels. Do not just think about what it represents; feel into it—charge it with the emotional nature of your work. Remember that if you are doing work to remove and banish energy, it is likely that the stone will retain part of that pattern, and it will be necessary to release it when the spell-work is done.

Making a Poppet

If there is no picture available of an individual you are working for (such as healing) or if that individual is not a specific person (such as work for love-drawing), you may want to employ the time-honored device of making a poppet. A poppet is a small rag doll you will charge to represent in individual. It need not be large or highly detailed; a simple doll made of handkerchiefs will do just fine.

You will need about 3 feet of cord or string (any kind will do) and two squares of material about 1 foot square—a handkerchief, piece of muslin, or even a paper towel will do. If you wish to get really personal, a scrap of the individual's clothing is a good choice. Take the crystal you have charged and wrap it in a small quantity of fabric or tissue so that you have a small, round ball about the size of a large marble. Place this in the center of the square of fabric and draw the fabric over it, cinching the fabric around it with the cord so the round object is enclosed as in a pouch. This is the poppet's head. Take the second square of cloth and make a short roll. This will be the poppet's arms. Divide the fabric below the head in two parts and place the roll tightly next to the tied cord. If you wish to put a charm or crystal at the heart center, place it in the center of the arm roll so that it will be tied into the torso of the poppet. You can use a cotton ball or wad of tissue wrapped around herbs and/or soaked with the oil you are using here. The choice of stuffing is up to you and will be part of the magical process of this creation. Whether you use a stone, crystal, charm, herbs, or other material, it should be calculated to link the poppet to the individual you are representing. Then, draw the two halves over the roll and wrap with cord again below the arms. With a crayon or other marking pen, draw a simple face on the head that represents the feeling you would like the individual to have. As you draw the face, imagine it is the face of the person it is intended to represent. Throughout the process of the work, know that this is not just a poppet, but is actually the person intended. The closer your intention and tie of reality is with the poppet, the more powerful your work will be.

You can even make a poppet to represent yourself to enhance your own personal work. Dress it with fabrics you would like to wear that connote the state or condition you would like to achieve. Put money in its pockets and draw a smile on its face. Even if the ritual will include burning the poppet, including a stone is all right. You will dispose of it with the ashes when you are done. But if your intention is burning, do not include any more nonflammable materials than you feel you must.

Spirit is the fifth element. It is present in all things as it is the essence of all Creation. It could be said that all the other

elements are simply states or conditions in which Spirit manifests on this plane. Spirit is what gives all things life and integrates them into the great harmony. Although the first four elements give your purpose its form and define its "shape," the whole must be infused with Spirit before it can take on the life and energy that will align it with you, and you with the essence of your goal in the Greater Universe. This is the point in your work where you will come to final clarity on exactly what it is you wish to achieve. Because the purpose of assembling the elements is to create a "mini-universe" of specifically tuned energies, something must stand for Spirit to give coherence and context to the other parts you have assembled. This is the element that gives consciousness to your process by formulating a specific statement, wish, or prayer that defines your goal.

This is a critical part of your magical process because it states exactly what you wish to occur as a result of your work. The written declaration is very much like an arrow, and the magical work surrounding it is like the bow that shoots the arrow. Both are very important if you wish to bring down your quarry. This is the time to analyze your desire and give it intellectual form. You should put some time and thought into deciding exactly what you want. Formulating such a statement is not something you should do on the spur of the moment. All too often our desires are fuzzy, unformed impulses. The purpose of this step is to clarify and specify your wish.

Because you are part of an infinitely powerful Universe, you have within you that same power to create and forge your reality. Thoughts have energy, impact, and power. What you think about and decide creates itself on a moment-to-moment basis whether or not you are consciously aware of this process. We are all constantly creating our lives, shaping our present and our future with our attitudes about ourselves, our relationships, and our surroundings. However, most of these decisions are not made freely and consciously. Instead, they are the result of unconscious programming. If circumstances in your life are not what you desire, it is necessary to change your act of creating what is undesirable to what is desirable. Thoughts are the actions of the inner self. What you think of yourself, your surroundings, and your interrelationships dictates from moment to moment their quality and their content. It dictates how you relate to life, how you either cope or don't cope. But thoughts are more than attitudes; they are forms of energy. The intensity and type of this energy acts upon its surroundings and, in turn, affects other energies it contacts. This is the part of the process in which you consciously turn that energy to form the reality you truly desire.

The Written Spirit

Spirit is represented by a written statement of your wish or intention. This is what unifies and organizes your spell-work, the focal point that unites all the others and moves them to your purpose. It is also a critical part of your mental process. Because writing is traditionally considered a powerful form of expression, writing down your wish or intention motivates you to clarify exactly what your goal is. Writing, in essence, makes ideas "real." Your intention should state your full legal name and birthday, as well as your intention, declaration, or petition. If you are working on behalf of someone else, it should include his or her full name and birthday, if it is known. It should include the day, date, and time you are working. A brief and precise statement of what your purpose is and a final closure that will set your stamp of will on it, such as "Amen" or "So mote it be," and your signature. Practice writing it out until you are certain that it states precisely what you need and want for the result of your spell. Take some time with this. Be careful what you wish for. When you are satisfied that it is clear and well phrased, print it out clearly. Copying it down in pen and ink will be part of the final ritual process.

Traditionally, this is done with a quill or staff pen, magical ink, and a piece of parchment. Parchment is expensive and not easy to come by. It can be just as effective to use a piece of good stationery that is bought and kept aside just for magical use. However, the choice of materials is up to the individual. A powerful spell can be written on a brown paper bag with a permanent marker or ballpoint pen. It is the clear will and intention of the writer that is the issue.

When you are done, you should fold the paper in thirds long ways, like a business letter, and in thirds again from side to side so that it makes a closed package. Be careful to fold the paper away from you if you are banishing, and toward you if you are drawing or commanding. Then, place it under the center candle to represent your object or wish. As a closing part of your work, you may wish to burn the paper to release the energy of your intention into the Greater Universe. Be sure that you have a metal or ceramic bowl that is large enough to contain the flame and that you do it in a safe place.

Magical Oils by Moonlight

The date, time, and moon phase when you are working.

I, (your full name), *born* (your birthday), *do declare, desire, and intend that* (state purpose here).

Amen! So mote it be!

Magical Inks

The final writing of the declaration is part of the spell-work itself. To write out your final declaration or petition, you should have a quill or staff pen that you use only for spell-work, and a piece of parchment. If you are not accustomed to writing with a staff pen or quill, you should practice with them first. They take a little getting used to so that the writing comes out clear and does not blot. The ink you choose should also be a magical one that is formulated for the particular purpose you have in mind.

Making your own magical ink is not as difficult as it sounds. Any regular black or colored ink (available at art supply stores in a wide variety of colors) can be made magical by adding a few drops of your oil blend to it and then letting it sit overnight. Be sure to add only a few drops, as more will compromise the quality of the ink and it may not be so easy to write with. If your oil is thick, such as frankincense, dilute it with alcohol or dypropylene glycol first. Your choice of color depends on the nature of your goal.

- Attraction—Red-Orange
- Blessing—Purple
- Cleansing and Banishing—Dark Purple
- Healing—Green
- Love—Pink or Rose
- Luck—Yellow
- Money—Green
- Prosperity—Green
- Protection—Red-Orange
- Psychic Enhancement—Turquoise
- Purging and Exorcising—Black
- Reversing—Black
- Success—Orange

There are also traditional magical inks that require a little more preparation—dragon's blood, bat's blood, and dove's blood. Please rest assured that bat's blood and dove's blood do not require any blood from a living creature any more than dragon's blood requires the blood of a dragon. These names are used descriptively for the power of the animal.

A word about quantity: Although these recipes are given in the traditional format of "parts" rather than specific measures, you must take into account that you need to make at least one batch equal to about 1/4 cup so that there will be enough depth in the bottle to dip the pen or quill. With this in mind, let your "parts" be at least 1 teaspoon and your yield will be between 1/4 and 1/3 cup. The specified drops of oil in the recipes will be appropriate to this quantity. If you want to make a larger batch, you will need to add more oil proportionately.

Dragon's Blood Ink

Dragon's blood ink is used for work involving strength, commanding, banishing, exorcising, purging, and controlling. Dragon's blood will greatly increase the energy of any formula to which it is added. Although it is tempting to put it in everything, remember that there is some work that does not require high energy. Psychic work, meditation, and healing sometimes require a more subtle approach.

- 1 part dragon's blood resin—finely ground.
- 1 part gum arabic—finely ground.
- 15 parts isopropyl (rubbing) alcohol, dypropylene glycol, or vodka.

Pour the resin and alcohol into a sealable jar, such as a canning jar. You should have just enough alcohol to cover the resin. Seal the jar. The resin will leach its color into the alcohol faster if it is a powder than if it is resin chunks. You may add 2 to 3 drops of dragon's blood oil to make it more fragrant if you wish. Let it steep until it is very dark. You may want to test it with a pen or toothpick on a piece of the paper you intend to use for your spell to see if it is dark enough. Allow it to dry before making your final decision, as it will get paler as it dries. When you are satisfied with the color, strain the ink through fine gauze or cheesecloth to remove any traces of resin that might remain. Put it in a brown bottle and store it away from the sun, as it will fade.

Dove's Blood Ink

Dove's blood ink is traditionally used for spells of increase and abundance, particularly love and attraction spells.

- 1 part dragon's blood resin—finely ground.
- 1 part gum arabic—finely ground.
- 2 drops cinnamon oil.
- 2 drops rose oil.
- 2 drops bay oil.
- 15 parts isopropyl (rubbing) alcohol, dypropylene glycol, or vodka.

Put the ground resins in the alcohol and steep them until they are dissolved. Now add the oils and ground gum arabic. Steep the solution until it turns dark, and then filter and bottle.

Bat's Blood Ink

Typically, bat's blood is for spell-work directed toward discord, tension, confusion, and havoc. The inclusion of myrrh in the formula gives it a strong banishing and purging effect. Use this formula when you want something **really gone**. But be warned that it may take other things along with it that are strongly connected to what you are banishing. Be sure to release all ties that are bound to what you find undesirable before doing this. You may also use the dragon's blood, myrrh, and cinnamon proportions in incense to purge a space.

- 4 part dragon's blood resin—finely ground.
- 1 part myrrh resin—finely ground.
- 2 drops cinnamon oil.
- 2 drops indigo coloring.
- 1 part gum arabic—finely ground.
- 24 parts isopropyl alcohol or dypropylene glycol.

Steep the powdered dragon's blood and myrrh resins in alcohol until they are dissolved. Add the cinnamon oil, Indigo coloring, and ground gum arabic. Steep the solution until dark, and then filter and bottle.

The Wish Spell and the Ritual

Chapter 9

ow that you have determined your purpose and the most beneficial time to set the forces in motion, you will need to choose your elements and transformation. It is time to assemble them and perform your magical spell. This is when all your thought and planning come to a point—like the arrow shot from the bow of your will. The first step in bringing all these elements together is to decide on a space to do this so that you will have a place to put the objects you will be using and so that you will have some peace and quiet while you are putting the spell in motion. This space can be the end or front of a bookshelf, a framed shadow box on the wall, a knick-knack shelf, or a trifle box. It need not be elaborate or large, but it should be in a place that will not be physically disturbed by others and where you can spend some private, quiet time. Be sure that it is large enough to accommodate your candles and incense burner safely. Your space does not even need to be inside a building. If you are more comfortable out of doors, or you have a special place of meditation in a garden or glade, doing your work there can amplify the energy you put into what you are doing by adding its quality of personal specialness to it.

At this point, it may even be helpful to have a checklist to be sure that you have thought of everything before the actual time for your working begins. It is particularly distracting to realize that at the last minute you have forgotten some small but crucial element, such as a lighter to light your candles or a pen and paper to write down what you learned from your divination before the recollection fades. The following is a suggested chain of events.

Your wish spell can be as simple as lighting a candle and stating your purpose at any time. But to bring your whole energy and focus to bear on your intention, it is a good idea to perform this in a more ritualized setting.

Sweep and clean the area you intend to use. You may use standard cleaning products with a few drops of blessing oil added to them or water with sea salt dissolved in it if you choose. Smudge and clear the space, then bless and seal it to your intended purpose.

Bathe with salt or smudge and cleanse yourself thoroughly. This will not only clear away any unwanted vibrations you have clinging to you, but should help you settle into a more centered and focused frame of mind.

Select and set up your elements one at a time. Begin with Air and move through the next four elements, arranging the items so that all of them can be reached easily. Be sure to put your candles at the back of the assembly so that you do not have to reach over a lit candle to reach the picture or incense burner.

Air: Incense with a scent corresponding to the purpose of your spell. You will need a holder for stick incense or a bowl of sand for charcoal and powdered incense.

Fire: You will need three candles: The center candle should be the same size or larger than the others to represent you, your goal, or the person for whom you are doing the spell. Two white guardian candles the same size or larger than the center candle should be set one on each side of the central candle. You will need holders for your candles or dishes to put them in, if necessary, and matches or a lighter.

Water: Have your ritual bath products made before you intend to use them. Bath salts or bath oil balls should be made ahead of time and placed on your altar so that you can bless them before you use them.

Earth: Picture, statue, crystal, or tarot card. If the picture is one that you wish to keep, such as a tarot card or family photograph, it is a good idea to use a photocopy of it instead of the original. This will become part of your magical process and should not be returned to daily use after your work is finished. Additionally, if you are working to release a person or situation, the paper or picture representing them should be burned at the close of your ritual. If you are using a stone or crystal, clear it before you begin the spell.

Spirit: Decide precisely what it is you wish beforehand. Practice writing it out and reading it back to yourself so that the wish is clear and contains all the details of the purpose you have in mind.

Once you have arranged your altar, sit down and take a deep breath. Relax and allow the stress and tensions of your life to fade into the background. Now is the time for your magic, not being concerned about mundane business. Breathe deeply and slowly and allow yourself to become focused on the items you have gathered. When you feel relaxed and focused, it is time to proceed.

Begin by invoking whatever Divine agency or spiritual help you feel would be the most beneficial to your purpose. Ask for guidance and protection while you work. Then, pick up the center candle, take the appropriate oil, and dress to anoint it. Briefly inscribe the purpose for which you are working, the date, and the phase of the Moon. Anoint each of the guardian candles beside it and inscribe the name of your guardian spirit or angel if you know it; if not, leave it blank. As you inscribe and oil each one, speak your wishes and purpose for it aloud. This is very important for clarifying and manifesting your wish in the physical Universe. When your candles are inscribed and dressed, light the center one, then the guardians. The purpose of the guardian candles is that, should your center candle be extinguished for any reason, you can relight it from one of their flames. This preserves the continuity of your work.

Once the candles are lit, light the incense. Make sure there is enough to make a smoke that you can see. Inhale this smoke deeply. Make sure it surrounds you and fills the space where you are working. Take the incense stick or bowl and pass it around your body and under your arms and legs. Allow the smoke from the incense to charge and cleanse your aura—your spiritual and physical energy fields to conform to your purpose.

When you have thoroughly cleansed and charged your energy fields with the scented smoke, focus on the center candle for a moment. Then, open the ink and take out the pen and paper. Copy the statement of your purpose that you have previously composed onto your special paper, including your name, your birthday, and the date and time you are working. It should look something like the model declaration in the section on Spirit (page 154). When you have finished writing it, read it aloud, speaking clearly and distinctly. This sets the forces in motion, so you want to do it firmly and clearly. Then, fold the paper into thirds the long way, but first make sure that if you wish to draw something to you, you fold the edge toward you; if you wish to banish something, fold with the edge going away from you. Now turn it and fold it into thirds down its length, folding either toward or away as before so that the paper makes an enclosed package. Place the folded statement beneath the center candle.

Now that the physical part of your spell is set up, you can begin your inner magic. You have prepared yourself and are focused on your intention. Take the photograph, picture, tarot card, or image representing your desire and place it where you can see it easily as you sit in meditation. Sitting comfortably in front of your altar, allow yourself to relax and become aware of the flickering light of the candles, the scent of the incense, and the sensations in your body. Sit quietly until you are comfortable and relaxed. Let your mind focus on the picture or image. Hold it in your mind. Reach out with your feelings and take the essence of the image inside you so that you surround the image. Experience its *reality*. Know that whatever your thoughts and intentions are, they have force, power, and reality. See this in your mind. Know that it exists and will manifest itself in your life and awareness. Know that your objective has already been achieved and is part of you. Sit for a while and allow the knowledge of this reality to become a comfortable part of your awareness. Meditate on this until the incense has completely burned. Take as long as you like. Light more incense if you would like to and continue with your meditation until you feel comfortable.

If part of your working is to take a magical bath, do so now. Once you have your images clearly in mind, fill the tub and steep yourself in the scented water. Allow the aroma to fill you with the essence of your purpose. On the final day of your work, or, if it is only a one-time process, take the paper you have written your intention on and the picture representing it and light them in the flame of the center candle. Drop them in the bowl and allow them to burn to ash. This will release the intention and energy you placed in them.

When your original work is complete, leave all the candles burning until they burn themselves out. The cycle of energy you have initiated must be allowed to complete its task. If your spell is intended to take more than one day, you should return to repeat your meditation each day at the same time. The guardian candles should burn longer than the others. If they burn quickly, and it appears that they will not last long enough, get another white candle and light it from the flame of the first one.

Reinforcing Your Intention

Once you have set the forces in motion with your wish ritual, you should set aside some time each day to visit your altar and meditate with it. Light the incense. As you look at the picture or image, focus on the intention you have set in motion in the Universe. Open your mind to the image and your goal until you can feel it all around you. Then sit quietly, allowing your mind to receive whatever impressions and guidance come to you at this time. Sometimes it will come quietly as a feeling of understanding or well-being, a lightening of your burden, or clarity of Spirit. Sometimes you may receive mental pictures or impressions. You may even feel as though you are receiving information that will be helpful to you in broadening your awareness of the project you have in mind. Whatever you feel, write down your impressions as clearly and completely as you can, along with the details of the work you are doing, what your goal is, what you have assembled, and when and how you meditate and focus on your goal. It will be helpful to keep a record or journal of these messages so that you can go over them later. Often, these meditations will bring some revelation that will help you towards your goal.

When the center candle has burned out, you may extinguish the others if they are still burning. Clean your altar space thoroughly again, and as you do so, acknowledge that your intention is manifesting in the Greater Universe and in your life. Feel the motion of the forces around you, bringing you and your goal closer to each other and manifestation in the physical Universe. Place whatever remains in a paper bag—wax drippings, incense ash, the ashes of your statement, and the picture. If your spell-work was intended as a blessing or drawing, you should keep these remaining elements of your spell-work. You may bury them in your yard if you have one, or keep them in a small container where you live. If your spell-work was one of banishing and reversing, put all the remnants of the spell in a paper

The Wish Spell and the Ritual

bag and carry them away from your house or property. Dispose of them appropriately and return to your house by a different way than the way you came.

Remember that in disposing of negative elements, you must be willing to release the negativity they represent. It will do you no good to go through an entire spell, working to banish a harmful person or situation from your life if you continue to recreate it in your thoughts and emotions. You must be ready to let the situation or individual go. Release them as you clean your altar and put your things away in a private place. Release them as you dispose of the wax and ashes. When you return home, know that you have started a new day in your life that is positive and strong. Those forces will no longer trouble you unless you yourself recreate the attachment to them. Your spell-work has planted the seeds of new beginnings, now you must nurture and cultivate what springs from them.

It is important at this time to remember that your objective will come about in a completely natural way. Each Universe must operate by its own natural laws. Nothing can exist or happen in any Universe that is in any way contrary to the laws that govern it. Be prepared to act when events change in your favor. You must follow up your magical work with action in the present-time reality. What you intend will come about within the laws of nature. Magic reveals and manifests itself over time in ways that are consistent with this Universe. This can be subtle and you may not notice your results at first. Or the changes may be very abrupt and noticeable. This is a good reason to keep a journal of your spell-work. Sometimes you may not even be aware of a change occurring until you look back on things and see how they have changed.

Un Rêve
des
Cathedrales

Chapter 10

T here will be times when your goal does not seem concrete enough to put into words; its essence may feel more like an undefined wish than a specific goal. You are saying, in effect, "If I knew what I wanted, there wouldn't be a problem." At such times, you need to step back a few paces and find a way to clarify your processes. There will also be times when your goal seems impossibly large—when a complete change of focus and perspective is necessary. At such times, a general and spiritual perspective may be a more workable path to your goal.

When you encounter such times, it may be a good idea to return to your study of the planetary energies, because for eons humankind has used the planets to categorize specific types of energy that are common to all humanity. These energies are called archetypes. The philosopher and psychologist Carl Jung discussed at great length how specific types and roles are common to all people all over the world, regardless of their social standing or religion. The Mother, for example, is something all peoples relate to. The Warrior, the King, the Sage, the Beautiful Lover, the Mischievous Opener of Ways are all common archetypes. We have created similar archetypes on a national level to personify the forces governing the countries we live in, such as Lady Liberty and Uncle Sam in the United States, and John Bull and Britannia in England. They are symbols of the national character of the people who live there and the embodiment of the ideals of those people.

For thousands of years the planets have served as a means to personify and categorize the conditions of human existence, our needs, and the forces operating in our lives as a way to better focus on them, understand and, perhaps, to deal with them. When you have no specific goal, but feel the need for changes in your life, it is a good thing to look at the planets and the deities they represent to perform a different kind of ritual so that you can draw these general energies into your life and consciousness. Because they are archetypes and can be generally categorized under the planets' energies, it is not difficult to find what "category" your need falls under, and then work through that energy in a ritual process to bring those energies into you life. This is a time when you may wish to focus on a particular deity or legendary figure from the many pantheons of gods from across time and around the world to use as your focus or ideal.

From the farthest reaches of time, human beings have equated the stars with the Divine energies and the gods who embody them. We know them as archetypes because they directly embody the basic elements of human life and behavior, and like human beings, they are multifaceted and show different aspects of the central primal energy. They represent an ideal of a particular quality of energy as well as the many ways in which that energy directs and expresses itself in our lives. When approaching a problem, it is good to look at the many faces each planet can display and attune your ritual process to coincide with that particular energy. Pluto rules regeneration and transformation, but it also rules addiction and obsession. It would be wise to specify what face of Pluto you want to address if you wish to transform your life. Transformation may be the order of the day, but you might wish to temper your process by specifying how much annihilation you are willing to go through to get to those desired changes. As another example, the Sun's energy brings life and health to all life, but it can burn and blast as well. For Egyptian Sekhmet, the destroyer is one face of this energy, while nurturing Bast, the cat-headed goddess of joy and beauty is another face of that energy. Before choosing a deity or energy to invoke, find out what specific properties you are looking for and focus on that as the direction of your work rather than calling down the "whole package" and letting the chips fall where they may.

As you may notice, not all the formulae in this text solely contain the herbs of the planet to which they pertain. That is because any energy is a compilation of several aspects that, taken together, create the whole picture. These oil formulae take the art of blending oils a step further. Not only are they composed of essential oils, they take other strength from natural whole herbs and stones that are placed in the bottles after the oils are formulated. This is because a whole herb contains trace elements that may not be present in the extracted oil. This process is call *maceration*. The oil leaches out the trace elements of the herbs over a period of time as it develops and matures, bringing an added depth to the formula. The addition of a stone to the oil gives it the extra charge of the stone's energy as well. You do not have to add large pieces of the stone, small chips will do unless otherwise noted. What you are looking for is the energy essence. Mix the oils first, then take a separate bottle, preferably one with a large-mouth opening, and put the herbs in the bottom with the stone, then pour the oil blend over them, making sure that all the herbs and stones are covered. Let the blend sit in a sunny window for at least seven days. Once a day, take the bottle and give it a shake to keep its contents mixed. This will encourage the elements of the herbs to mix with the liquid essences. Take some time to sit with your oil and meditate your purpose for it. Allow the charge of your intention to permeate the bottle and its contents. In doing so, you will be setting up a powerful resonance even before your actual spell-work begins. Seven days will give it time to develop its full character. The warmth of the sunlight coming in the window will help in this process.

Sun—
Dispelling the Darkness

Apollo was the Greek god of the Sun. He was worshipped as the god of healing as well as divination. While this may seem a far stretch at first, by taking a closer look we see that, in all his aspects, he ruled over the forces that drive away darkness and shadows. In healing, he drives away the darkness of disease; in divination, he drives away the shadows of ignorance and uncertainty by guiding us through the dark and hidden realms. In many cultures, this aspect of driving away the darkness equates the Sun with healing. The Egyptian lion-headed goddess Sekhmet personified the burning, fierce heat of the Sun and was also credited with bringing disease and pestilence. She also had the power to heal diseases, and the first-known college of physicians was founded in her temple in ancient Memphis. In addition to being a fearsome warrior aspect, her powers were never exerted without cause. It was she who drove out the demons of darkness and restored Creation to order.

The power of the Sun drives away our inner darkness. Whether it stems from fear or pain, the Sun brings light to dark places. Look to the Sun when you are facing issues of inner uncertainty to find courage and confidence, and to bring order to your life when the forces of chaos become too extreme. Also, look to the Sun when Winter has gone on too long in your life, whether in the real-world sense of needing a lift from Winter's short gray days, or in the metaphorical sense of life being hard, depressing, unprofitable, and unfulfilling. The Sun can restore the brightness in our outlook, and consequently, can bring in the forces of attraction, renewal, and success. It can bring a healing balm to the pain of grief and loss. Use orange candles to focus this energy.

Apollo was also the God of Truth. Invoke his energy to see through the shadows of any situation, resolve confusion, and sort out lies and falsehood. If you suspect that someone is double-dealing you, ask the Sun to show the truth of the matter. Also ask the Sun for help if someone is damaging your reputation. The Sun is about your public face—not only how you see yourself, but also how others see you. If you are the target of malicious gossip and falsehood, the Sun could be your best ally in setting things right.

The oil formula for the Sun's energy is transformative. While protecting the user, it banishes darkness and negativity, and it brings success and prosperity in its wake. Ask the Sun's energy for healing of body, mind, and spirit, and to find the way to your true self.

Sun ☉

- 1 part **bay** (Fire ☉)—transformation, protection, dispels negativity
- 4 parts **orange** (Fire ☉)—attracts material prosperity, beauty, attraction
- 2 parts **cinnamon** (Fire ☉)—protection, uplifting, creativity, luck
- 1 part **frankincense** (Fire ☉)—banishing, protection, strength, uplifting
- **Herbs:** 2 parts **mistletoe** (Fire ☉)—banishing, protection, reversing, luck
- 1 part **rowan** (Fire ☉)—healing, power, protection, resistance, success
- **Stone: carnelian**—courage of the heart

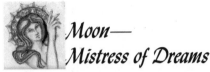

Moon—
Mistress of Dreams

Diana, the huntress, was Apollo's sister. She personified the feminine, emotional inner nature. In life we are all seeker and hunter of something. Our emotions are the senses of the Spirit, and the Moon heightens these senses to enable us to find what we need. Diana was also the protector of mothers and all young creatures. The fluid nature of the Moon allows us to relax, and through our higher awareness, see through illusion. It breaks up old energy forms with its cycling transformative nature so that we can create what we wish. In Egypt, the god Thoth was associated with the Moon. He was the scribe, mathematician, and magician. His wisdom of mathematical laws and probabilities bring us the power to change what we find—remove our limitations, and, by seeing through the darkness at last, to hunt down our quarry. Burn a white or silver candle for the Moon energy to get in touch with your emotional senses and cast off old illusions.

Moon ☽

- 1 part **lemon** (Water ☽)—love, purification, clarity, calming
- 2 parts **lotus** (Water ☽)—higher awareness, sensuality, relaxing
- 4 parts **gardenia** (Water ☽)—protection, hex-breaking
- 1 part **jasmine** (Water ☽)—dreams, uplifting, love, wealth
- **Herbs:** 1 part **hibiscus flower** (Water ☽)—clairvoyance, balancing
- 1 part **orchid flower** (Water ♀)—balance, inner beauty
- **Stone: staurolite**—dispels illusions, protection, wealth, control of the four elements, compassion, spirituality, release

Mercury—
Quick-Footed Opener of Ways

Mercury was the messenger of the Greek gods. His shoes had wings to carry him instantly wherever he was needed. Consequently, he presides over communication and travel. When you are on the road, invoke Mercury to help you with your journey so it will be trouble-free and your luggage will not get lost. Ask him for help with your communications, whether you are mailing something important or you want to be sure what you are saying is heard and understood. He can help you be efficient as well as articulate. His Divine nature breaks through all opposition whether mental or physical. When your mind is in a muddle, ask Mercury for help. If you are studying for a test, he can help you stay clear and focused so that you will retain and express the material fully and clearly. If you are preparing a presentation, Mercury can help make sure all the details are covered and that it is presented in the best possible way. Like the elephant-headed Hindu god Ganesh, he will open the way for you to find wisdom, quick wits, and a clear head. Mercury was also a playful trickster and thief, and there are many stories of his escapades with the other gods. But it is his nature to show you the way through your difficulties by pointing out your weaknesses. It is also the Mercury energy that will deal with thieves in your life. Invoke Mercury when someone is taking what is yours, whether it is physical property or your reputation and place in life. Mercury will ferret out a thief and show him for what he truly is. But when invoking Mercury, you will have to pay attention. His tricks will show you where your life is most in need of work to open the way for the places you wish to go. And his mischievous nature will show you the flaws in your plans. If you pay attention, this can be a valuable aid in catching trouble before it catches you. Burn a yellow candle for Mercury energy to clear your head and point the way.

Mercury ☿

- 1 part **clove** (Air ☿)—strength, uplifting, luck, overcoming opposition
- 1 part **peppermint** (Air ☿)—psychic powers, release, transformation
- 1 part **almond** (Air ♀)—alertness, wisdom
- **Herbs: 2 parts red azalea flower** (Air ☿)—clarity
- 1 part **mandrake** (American mandrake will do) (Fire ☿)—protection, power
- 1 part **elecampane** (Air ☿)—love, protection, psychic powers
- **Stone: topaz** or **honey calcite**—mental acuity, flexibility, brightness, uplifting

Venus—
Queen of Attraction

All across the globe, the beautiful morning star has been associated with the queen of love and beauty. She rules all forms of love and pleasure, all beautiful things, and all the people who create them. Artists, musicians, actors, clothing designers, jewelers, chefs, gardeners, and florists—all the people whose lives are centered on the creation of beautiful and pleasant things are under her care. Venus is about unifying the power of the heart with the power of creative potential. She is known as the Queen of love and joy. The keynote of Venus is attraction. Lady Venus attracts whatever delights you, whether that is the satisfaction of creativity, the pleasures of luxury, or the joys of love and sensuality. She can help you find your own inner beauty and joy. When working with Venus, burn a green or rose candle to tell her your objective. Venus can help you break the chains of feeling unworthy and incapable. Ask her to help you through an artistic block you may be having. But you must be ready to let go of your inner barriers in order to accept what she brings you. She can help you through your inhibitions to find the romantic lover or the artist in yourself, and to cultivate the pleasures of beauty and luxury in your life. Burn green and rose candles for Venus to bring fulfillment and pleasure to your life.

Venus ♀

- 2 parts **frangipani** (Water ♀)—attraction, love, base and heart chakras
- 1 part **rose geranium** (Fire ♂)—blessing, hex-breaking, uplifting, liberating, protection, passion
- 1 part **honeysuckle** (Fire ☉ and ♂)—luck, psychic powers, fidelity, relaxing, peace
- **Herbs:** 1 part **coltsfoot** (Water ♀)—peace, love, visions
- 1 whole **bing cherry** (not maraschino) (Air ♀)—gain, love, fertility
- **Stone: watermelon tourmaline** (or a mixture of rose and green tourmaline)—love, passion

Earth— Mother of Manifestation

The power of the third planet from the Sun—Earth—is most often overlooked. Mother Earth has brought us forth and it is from the bounty of her air, earth, and waters that we are fed and nurtured. Earth magic is about optimism and feeling safe and secure. If you are looking for your place in life, look to Earth to find balance and perspective, and your inner feeling of your place in the scheme of things—your "rightness of being." Burn a brown candle for Earth in order to feel the strength and power that are always yours, and to connect to its seemingly bottomless bounty.

Earth ⊗

- 2 parts **magnolia** (Earth ♀)—love, fidelity, purity, psychic powers
- 2 parts **hyacinth** (Earth ☉)—happiness, love, optimism
- 2 parts **lavender** (Air ☿)—love, protection, strength, balance
- 2 parts **dragon's blood** (Fire ♀ or ♂)—protection, power
- **Herbs:** I part **white rose petals** (Air ♀)—inner peace, good luck
- I part **pine needles** (Fire ♂)—banishing, cleansing, love, prosperity, protection, regeneration, strength
- **Stone: brown agate**—strength, grounding

Mars— Warrior of Passion

The shield of Mars will protect you, as his sword will strike through to the heart of any difficulty. More than force, Mars rules passion. His is the force of will that drives through to the heart of any project. But Mars is more than his warrior face. Besides the warrior and gladiator that we see so often, Mars is also the grail knight, pursuing his quest with bravery and a stout heart that casts out doubt in the face of adversity. It is the power of Mars that encourages us to follow our dreams and our quests through all the dark places of life. His strong sword vanquishes the perils of the journey as his true, passionate heart holds the image of the quest. Mars may be Julius Caesar, but he is also Lancelot and Galahad. He gives us the courage to follow our dreams and the power to forge them into reality. The ardor of his heart is unconquerable even in the face of our greatest trials.

Invoke Mars when you want to become more independent and self-directed and when you need to reach deep within yourself to find the strength of heart to manifest your goals into reality. You may meet some opposition to this idea, not only from others, but from within yourself, and it is Mars that will unlock the passion within to cast out the shadows of doubt and difficulty. Attune yourself to Mars energy to reinforce your personal energy and to help remove any hidden barriers you may have within yourself that might prevent you from achieving your goal in a healthy and positive way. Mars energy is not always the military force associated with Roman Ares. There are many other images that incorporate the concept of the Mars energy that bring other essences to bear along with it. As your central focus, you might choose an image of Athena. She was not only a self-sufficient warrior figure, but also widely praised for her wisdom, rationality, beauty, and skill at domestic arts. Or you might wish to focus on Galahad when you are following a dream. While they are all consummate warriors, a more subtle approach might better serve your process.

Burn a red candle to invoke the power of Mars to find the passion to drive your life through to its determined goal.

Mars ♂

- ♣ I part **dragon's blood** (Fire ♀ or ♂)—power, protection, banishing, love
- ♣ 2 parts **allspice** (Earth ♀)—strength of will
- ♣ I part **ginger** (Fire ♂)—healing, energizes, passion, power, strength, prosperity
- ♣ **Herbs:** I part **damiana** (Earth ♀)—increase power, passion, sensuality
- ♣ I **hot red pepper**—power, energy
- ♣ **Stone:** red jasper—strength of force

Jupiter— Powerful All-Father

Jupiter represents the powerful king, who rules of all the gods. All the attributes of the great and benevolent king come through Jupiter, whether it is largesse and riches, or law and justice. He has a strong urge to purify, sanctify, and bless. When seeking justice in legal matters or just fair play in general, Jupiter is the energy to invoke. He can see through complicated matters and bring about equitable solutions to the most complex of matters. He also rules favors and blessings of all kinds. When you are seeking to impress your boss and find advancement in your profession, Jupiter can help. He does not give his blessings idly, but instead insists that you earn your place. But if you have earned something rightly, Jupiter will give you the energy behind your search for advancement. Burn a purple candle for his royal majesty.

Jupiter ♃

- ♣ I part **hyssop** (Earth ☉)—anointing, creativity, mental powers, protection, prosperity
- ♣ 2 parts **sage** (Air ♃)—consecration, purifying, protection, retention, strength, wisdom
- ♣ I part **clove** (Fire ☉)—dispel negativity, hex-breaking, protection, mental powers, protection, purification
- ♣ **Herb:** I part **anise** (Air ☿ and ♃)—purification, protection, money, good luck, divination
- ♣ **Stone: sugulite**—mental powers, psychic powers, strength of Spirit

Saturn— Time and Wise Teacher

Saturn was also called Chronos, Father Time, and he is the great teacher of life's lessons. While many people look on his lessons as painful, Saturn is all about the lessons learned by time and a full life. Life brings its own share of trials and tribulations, as well as rewards and achievements. Saturn will help you see through the tangle of events to find the pattern and the lesson to learn so that you become stronger and wiser, and he will help you find the inner rewards of achievements as well as the limitations of time and circumstance. Remember, not only does time *dis*solve all things but can *re*solve them as well. As such, Saturn rules the elderly, whether they have become wise and sage through the years or have become a burden through infirmity and declining abilities. Saturn deals with heritage and legacies. These are all the things that come through the passage of time, whether they are the heritage of a family or people or the actual inheritance that comes through a will or bequest. He also rules ancestral lands and family heirlooms. If you are in a dispute about inheritance, ask Saturn to straighten it out, and with it, the relationship you have with your relatives.

This also implies that Saturn rules issues that come through a family line, such as inherited disorders and dysfunctions. You inherit more than eye color and body type from your parents. Through them you have inherited an entire set of attitudes and abilities, the strengths and the weaknesses that come from your upbringing. They are yours to draw on—to transmute and then to pass onto your own family. The way in which you deal with them determines how they will affect the ones that come after you, and Saturn can help you put into perspective the scars from your early life so that they will not limit you in your future, so you will not pass them on to those around you. Invoke Saturn in matters related to your karma, that is, the unresolved issues you have accrued over time from lifetime to lifetime. If you feel trapped in a vicious cycle that seemingly has no end or solution, if painful patterns keep repeating endlessly in your life, perhaps it is time to ask Saturn what lesson you have yet to learn from it. Ask him to clarify what you need to do to resolve the pattern so that you can go on to better things and new ventures. All things happen in your life for a reason, and Saturn holds the key to resolving old issues that continue to plague you. Burn an indigo candle for Saturn for the lessons of life and the ages.

Saturn ♄

- 1 part **cypress** (Earth ♄)—longevity, mental powers and acuity
- 3 parts **chamomile** (Water ☽)—material wealth and well-being, meditation
- 4 parts **carnation** (Fire ☉)—blessing, protection, stimulant, strength
- Herb: 1 part **mugwort** (Air ♀)—psychic powers, dreams, visions, psychic protection, divination, rest, strength
- 1 part **patchouli** (Earth ♄)—psychic protection, clairvoyance, exorcism, hex-breaking, grounding
- Stone: **chrysocholla**—reach beyond personal limitations and old constructs, healing inner wounds

Uranus— Electrical Father of Invention

Uranus was the first sky-god and is called the Father of all Creation with his mate, Gaia, Mother Earth. Together they gave birth to all Creation. As such, he is now credited with being the Father of all invention and new things. In our age, this is particularly associated with electrical devices, nuclear power, and airplanes and airline travel. If you are an inventor, and your new project will not come together, ask Uranus for help. He can show you the inner mystery that will resolve your deadlock. He is also said to help with all electrical devices. He rules computers and cell phones and all the gadgets we rely on in our daily life from microwave ovens to Palm Pilots. He can help you find the bug in your program or the glitch in your system. He can help your system remain stable when the going gets critical. Burn a pearlescent or amber candle for Uranus to unlock your curiosity and inventive potential and keep your computer running right.

Uranus ♅

- 4 parts **amber** (Water ♀)—attraction, love, happiness, protection, strength
- 2 parts **benzoin** (Air ♀)—hex-breaking, exorcism, dispel negativity, prosperity, peace of mind, wisdom, protection
- 2 parts **primrose** (Air ♀)—love, protection, spirituality, truth
- **Herb:** 1 part **copal** (Fire ♃)—hex-breaking, exorcism, dispel negativity, protection, consecration, increase power, contact other planes
- 1 part **lemongrass** (Air ☿)—fidelity, passion, uplifting, growth, psychic development
- **Stone: moldavite**—connection to celestial energies, other plane energies

Neptune— Master of Inspiration and Secrets

As master of the ocean depths, Neptune rules all secrets and things hidden in dark, unreachable places. He is pictured as a giant merman and, as such, he can go to those depths for you and reveal what is hidden, in yourself or in the world around you. He swims to the darkest depths and brings his treasure up to the surface of the sparkling waves. His is a dual world of silence and mystery, and sparkling revelation. His actions are within your inner self rather than in the visible outer world. He rules unconsciousness as well as illumination. He can bring brilliant flashes of inspiration and insight. Neptune can help you tear away the veils of self-delusion so that you can find the truth about yourself. He can help you face and overcome the roots of addictions and harmful escapism.

Neptune's hidden world rules covert activities and spying as well as fraud and deceit. Neptune works well with Apollo to bring these to the surface and expose deception and lies. You may also invoke him in circumstances where what you are doing needs to remain hidden, and in burying things that you wish never to be known. His realm holds all things psychic, mystical, and occult. Look to Neptune to help you develop your psychic talents and explore your inner mysteries. Burn a turquoise candle for inspiration and to reveal what is hidden.

Neptune ♆

- 2 parts **vetivert** (Earth ♀)—strength, commanding, increase power, good luck, grounding, prosperity, protection
- 1 part **rosemary** (Fire ☉)—transformation, protection, hex-breaking, happiness, courage, confidence, mental powers, uplifting, endings
- 2 parts **sweetgrass** (Air ♀)—attunement, spirituality, calling spirits
- 3 parts **pine** (Fire ♂)—banishing, cleansing, love, prosperity, protection, regeneration, strength
- **Herb:** 1 part **lemon peel** (Water ☽)—love, purification, clarity, calming
- 1 part **dandelion** leaves (Air ♃)—psychic powers, wishes, divination
- **Stone:** lapis lazuli—divination, connection to celestial energies

Pluto— Transformer

Pluto is the Roman name for the Greek god of the Underworld, Hades. His action is a dual one of annihilation and regeneration. His action is extreme and will sweep away circumstances with a broad hand to clear the way for a new cycle to begin. This is not a safe or comfortable thing to do, and the forces he represents can be extreme. He rules the forces of destiny—how we choose to live our lives, whether we choose the forces of regeneration or degeneration, whether we choose to embrace our lives or deny them. There are times when all other avenues of approach have failed and a situation has become so untenable that all that is left is to remove it altogether. As a last resort, appeal to Pluto to initiate an entire change of cycle. But be advised that the action of Pluto will sweep all away—the good with the bad. When invoking Pluto, be ready to completely reconstruct your life.

Pluto is also in charge of banishing and exorcisms. Dark energies that are ingrained in any situation can be sent back to Pluto for him to deal with. His are the Spirits that have become stuck on this plane and no longer have a useful place here. Pluto can break through rigid energy patterns and negative energy to set you and the situation free. He will transform the situation so that you can then reconstruct the energies in a more positive framework.

Burn a black and red candles for Pluto and use bat's blood ink to write your declaration for transformation and rebirth.

Pluto ♇

- 4 parts **sandalwood** (Water ☽)—spirituality, protection, wisdom, harmony, balance
- 1 part **myrrh** (Fire ☉)—hex-breaking, protection, transformation, success, endings, exorcism, uplifting
- 1 part **frankincense** (Fire ☉)—banishing, protection, strength, uplifting
- 2 parts **heliotrope** (Fire ☉)—banish barriers, exorcism
- Herb: 1 part **cumin** seed (Fire ♂)—banishing, dispel negativity, protection, reversing
- 1 part **elder flower** (Water ♀)—banishing, protection, exorcism, emotional healing, sleep
- **Stone: obsidian**—protection or personal energies, reversing

All the Peoples of the World

These planetary energies exist in nearly every culture on Earth. Their faces are as numerous as there are people who recognize them.

But each culture has its own particular viewpoint on these energies. To focus your process further, it might be well for you to investigate the mythologies of the world, and, when picking a specific energy that you wish to draw upon, find a god or goddess who embodies the qualities you wish to draw upon most closely. The following chart lists a few of the major deities from some of the most well-known world pantheons, but there are many more. A trip to the library to find the one that most closely resonates with your Spirit and goal would be well worth the effort.

	Hindu	Yoruba/ Santeria	Egyptian	Norse	Greek	Roman
Venus	Sarvasvati/ Lakshmi	Oshun	Hathor	Freya	Aphrodite	Venus
Sun	Surya	Olofi	Horus	—	Apollo	Apollo
Mars	Kali/Shiva/ Agni	Ogun	Sekhmet	Tyr	Ares/ Minerva	Mars
Jupiter	Ganesha	Chango	Amon-ra	Thor	Zeus	Jupiter
Saturn	Yama/ Durga	Oya	Anubis	—	Chronus	Saturn
Earth	Tara	Yemaya	Isis	Frigga	Demeter/ Gaia	Hera
Underworld	—	—	Osiris	—	Hades	Pluto
Ocean	—	Olokun	—	—	Poseidon	Neptune

Invoking the Divine—
The Power of the God and Goddess

God and Goddess represent the polarities of the Divine balance. We see them in our own lives first as Father and Mother, living embodiments of strength and nurturing. We recognize them as the source of our life and our continued existence. We see them as the providers of food, shelter, love, and guidance. As we grow older, we grow in our awareness of our physical parents to see them as more complex human beings; like ourselves, they have the same shortcomings and limitations, as well as the same strengths and desires. But our awareness of the complimentary yet opposing archetypes they represented in our infancy remains—a consciousness of the all-pervasive Father and Mother who look over all Creation as their children. Sometimes, these are personified as Father Sky and Mother Earth. They are the core essence from which all other concepts and faces of the Divine sprang. All gods and goddesses are aspects of their nature, but at the center, they are Father and Mother. There are times when we feel the need to reconnect with their energy. We find our own identity in their nature. Aspects of each are resident in every person regardless of gender for we are not one-sided beings, but complex interactions of all the forces. In another sense, God represents our outward dominant face, our personality, and the way we relate to the world. God energies are those we use to interface with the physical world and to have our needs met. He is the Hunter/Warrior in all of us. The Goddess represents our inner emotional nature, our sensitivities and the way we express those qualities. It is the Goddess in each of us that is the dreamer. Holding the seeds in our emotional and mental womb until they can be born and thrive. It takes both expressions of energy to create our lives from moment to moment. They live in the Greater Universe as conscious entities, but they also live within each of us as part of the fabric of our being.

In many traditions, each deity is represented in three different aspects, representing the phases of human life and development. For the God, these faces are Youth, Warrior, and Sage. For the Goddess, these faces are Maiden, Mother, and Crone. Each has much to teach as each we find resident within ourselves.

Invoking the God Energy

The energy of the God represents the universal masculine principle—the Yang principle that is aggressive, active, and extroverted. Each of his aspects relates to his role as seeker, defender, and provider. As the Youth he is the Trickster, full of pranks and joyful discovery. His energy is boundless as he explores the world around him, getting into mischief and amusing everyone. It is by this mischief that he discovers the nature of his world. Turn to the energy of the Divine Youth when you want to break free of the boundaries of your world and find the joy of discovery and each new day inside you. As the Warrior, he is the protector and provider, warrior and hunter. He is also the passionate Lover and Mate of the Goddess. It is by his tenderness and passion that life is fertilized within the Mother that would otherwise remain unrealized potential. It is by our passions that we bring forth from ourselves our own inner potential and make our dreams into realities. The Father has his tender side as well, because he loves his children and wants what is best for them in life. Sometimes his teaching is stern, but the end in mind is that each of us learn what we need in order to become strong and healthy adults. Turn to the Warrior for protection and defense and to ask that he show you how best to hunt down and gather all that you need to make your life strong and secure. Let him teach you how to turn your potential into strength. In his old age, the God is a Teacher and Sage who provides us with his wisdom and counsel, gleaned from years of living and learning through experience. The strong arm of the Warrior combines with the role of teacher and is now turned to the dispensing of Justice. Ask the Sage for advice and wisdom, and to help you find what is just in any situation.

Light a gold, red, or black candle for the God and focus on whatever aspect of his nature would be most helpful to you in securing your daily life. As you mix the oil, concentrate on each separate power the essences represent. You will call on all his aspects as you add the ingredients one by one.

God-Invoking Oil

- 5 parts **dragon's blood** (Fire ♀ or ♂)—power, protection, banishing, love

- 2 parts **orange** (Fire ☉)—attracts material prosperity, beauty, attraction

- 2 parts **carnation** (Fire ☉)—blessing, protection, stimulant, strength

- 1 part **juniper** (Fire ☉)—centering, purification, retention, strength, secrets, gain

- **Herbs:** 1 part **damiana** (Earth ♀)—increase, increase power, passion, sensuality

- 1 part **coltsfoot** (Water ♀)—love, visions, peace

- I cranberry (Fire ☉)—calming, healing, defense, protection, uplifting
- **Stones: citrine** and **carnelian**—courage of the heart, strength of spirit

Invoking the Goddess Energy

The aspects of the Goddess—Maiden, Mother, and Crone—all relate to her nature as a life-giver. She is the universal feminine, the Yin principle that is passive, peaceful, and introspective. And, in truth, it is with our inner emotional nature that we dream our dreams and create our world. Without these dreams, the strength of the Warrior lacks purpose and becomes violence and destruction. As a Maiden, the Goddess represents Spring, when the world is new and full of promise. She is a delicate, joyful creature, full of play and renewal. When Winter has set in your heart too long, ask the Maiden to bring Spring back to your Spirit. As the Mother, the Goddess is abundant and creative. She is the Queen of dreams, and it is by the Mother aspect that we gestate the seeds of our potential and bring it forth to be born into our world. The Mother is the embodiment of nurturing love—endlessly patient and forgiving. Ask the Mother to help you with your feelings and dreams, because if these are denied, your world will be barren and lifeless. The Crone has lived into old age, gathering knowledge and wisdom. She has seen dreams born into reality and knows how best to integrate them into the fabric of life for the betterment of the community at large. Ask the Crone about the nature of strength through service. The Crone also prepares us for the final dream of transition: death. She is the keeper of the gateway between the worlds and moderates the passage between. Invoke the Crone for knowledge of the wider Great Universe that is only beyond the doorstep of this one.

Burn a silver, green, or black candle for the Goddess to bring her loving, creative, life-affirming nature into your life.

Goddess-Invoking Oil

- I part **honeysuckle** (Fire ☉ and ♂)—luck, psychic powers, fidelity, relaxing, peace
- I part **jasmine** (Water ☽)—dreams, uplifting, love, wealth
- I part **lotus** (Water ☽)—higher awareness, sensuality, relaxing

- 2 parts **vanilla** (Water ♀)—calming, relaxing, passion, mental powers
- 5 parts **gardenia** (Water ☽)—love, peace, spirituality, heart chakra
- **Herbs:** 1 part **red** or **pink rose** petals (Air ♀)—love, beauty, harmony, balance, good luck, consecration
- 1 part **heather** (Water ♀)—good luck, protection
- 1 part ground **allspice** (Earth ♀)—strength of will
- **Stone:** moonstone—inner peace, psychic powers, focus

The Unity of Spirit

Beyond the diverse aspects of the planets, even beyond the Divine Duality that is God and Goddess, is the One Divine Spirit. This is the one light of the Universe that embodies all without difference or separation. It shines through every creature and unifies all Creation. There are times in our lives when we simply need to acknowledge the presence of that light within us, to reconnect our focus with the Divine Presence and find that light shining through our hearts. This is the energy that will bless any enterprise, because all things flow from it. It will consecrate any place and fill it with the radiance that is all things. Light a single white candle to meditate on the beauty of the presence of the Divine Spirit in your life.

Divine Spirit Oil

- 1 part **carnation** (Fire ☉)—blessing, protection, stimulant, strength
- 1 part **lotus** (Water ☽)—higher awareness, sensuality, relaxing
- 1 part **honeysuckle** (Fire ☉ and ♂)—luck, psychic powers, fidelity, relaxing, peace
- 3 parts **lemongrass** (Air ♀)—fidelity, honesty, passion, refreshing, uplifting, psychic development
- **Herb:** 1 whole **clove** (Fire ☉)—dispel negativity, hex-breaking, protection, mental powers, protection, purification
- 1 part **eyebright** (Air ☉)—mental clarity and acuity, psychic powers, memory
- **Stone:** quartz point—harmony, balance, clarity, focus

Appendix A:
List of Oils by Property

Abundance and Prosperity

ATTRACTION
Bay — Fire ☉
Sweet Pea — Water ♀

ATTRACTION— FRIENDS AND CUSTOMERS
Mistletoe — Fire ☉
Peony — Fire ☉
Citronella — Fire ♃
Linden — Air ♃

ATTRACTION (MAGNETISM)
Orange Blossom — Fire ☉

ATTUNEMENT
Sweetgrass — Air ♀

BLESSING
Carnation — Fire ☉
Rose Geranium — Fire ♂

COMMANDING
Basil — Fire ♂
Calamus — Earth ♀
Camphor — Water ☽
Catnip — Air ♀

Civet — Fire ☉
Galangel — Fire ♂
Marigold — Fire ☉
Menthol — Fire ♂
Musk — Earth ♀
Mustard — Fire ♂
Orris — Earth ♀
Patchouli — Earth ♃
Poppy — Water ☽
Safflower — Fire ☉
Saffron — Fire ☉
Spikenard — Earth ♃
Vetivert — Earth ♀

CONFIDENCE
Rose Geranium — Fire ♂
Rosemary — Fire ☉

DRAWING
Sweet Pea — Water ♀

EMPOWER
Redwood — Earth ⊗

GAIN
Acacia — Fire ☉
Agrimony — Fire ♃
Angelica — Fire ☉
Caraway — Air ☿
Cedar (Cedarwood) — Fire ♃
Cherry — Air ♀
Juniper — Fire ☉
Mistletoe — Fire ☉
Mustard — Fire ♂
Poppy — Water ☽

GOOD LUCK
Agrimony — Fire ♃
Allspice — Earth ♀
Anise — Air ☿
Bay — Fire ☉
Bayberry — Earth ☿
Bindweed — Earth ♄
Cassia (Cinnamon) — Fire ☉
Cinquefoil (Five Finger) — Fire ♃
Clover — Air ☿
Galangel — Fire ♂

Heather	Water	T
Honeysuckle	Fire	♂
Linden	Air	♃
Marigold	Fire	☉
Mistletoe	Fire	☉
Morning Glory	Earth	♄
Musk	Earth	♀
Myrrh	Fire	☉
Nutmeg	Fire	♃
Orange	Fire	☉
Peach	Water	♀
Peony	Fire	☉
Peppermint	Fire	☿
Persimmon	Water	♀
Pineapple	Fire	♂
Poppy	Water	☽
Rose	Air	♀
Rose, White	Air	♀
Rosemary	Fire	☉
Strawberry	Water	♀
Vetivert	Earth	♀
Vetivert	Earth	♀
Violet	Water	♀
Water Lily	Water	☽

HAPPINESS

Amber	Water	♀
Apple Blossom	Water	♀
Basil	Fire	♂
Cherry Blossom	Water	♀
Dittany	Earth	♀
Hyacinth	Earth	☉
Jasmine	Water	☽
Lemon Verbena	Air	♀
Lily of the Valley	Air	☿
Marigold	Fire	☉
Marjoram	Air	☿

Myrrh	Fire	☉
Orange	Fire	☉
Orange, Mandarin	Fire	☉
Peppermint	Fire	☿
Rosemary	Fire	☉
Safflower	Fire	☉
Saffron	Fire	☉
Spearmint	Air	♀
Strawberry	Water	♀
Violet	Water	♀

MANIFESTATION

Oakmoss	Water	☽
Material Objects		
Agrimony	Fire	♃
Almond	Air	♀
Basil	Fire	♂
Bayberry	Earth	☿
Bergamot	Fire	☉
Bindweed	Earth	♄
Cedar (Cedarwood)	Fire	♃
Chamomile	Water	☽
Cinquefoil (Five Finger)	Fire	♃
Clary Sage	Earth	☿
Honeysuckle	Fire	U
Hyssop	Fire	♃
Jasmine	Water	☽
Mandrake	Fire	☿
Morning Glory	Earth	♄
Myrrh	Fire	☉
Orange	Fire	☉
Peppermint	Fire	☿
Poppy	Water	☽
Vervain	Earth	♀

MONEY

Acacia	Fire	☉
Agrimony	Fire	V
Almond	Air	♀
Anise	Air	☿
Basil	Fire	♂
Bay	Fire	☉
Bergamot	Fire	☉
Bindweed	Earth	♄
Galangel	Fire	♂
Morning Glory	Earth	♄

OPTIMISM

Heliotrope	Fire	☉
Hyacinth	Earth	☉
Lily of the Valley	Air	☿
Persimmon	Water	♀
Raspberry	Water	☽

OVERCOME OPPOSITION

Asafoetida	Earth	♄
Bay	Fire	☉
Clover	Air	☿
Valerian	Earth	☿
Wormwood	Fire	♂

POWER

Dragon's Blood	Fire	♀
Ginger	Fire	♂
Hemlock	Water	♄
Mandrake	Fire	☿
Obeah	Fire	♃
Van-Van	Earth	♀

PROSPERITY/MONEY

Agrimony	Fire	♃
Allspice	Earth	♀
Almond	Air	♀

Balsam, Fir	Air	☿
Banana	Water	♀
Basil	Fire	♂
Bayberry	Earth	☿
Benzoin	Air	♀
Bergamot	Fire	☉
Bindweed	Earth	♄
Blue Bonnet	Air	☿
Camelia	Water	☽
Cedar (Cedarwood)	Fire	♃
Chamomile	Water	☽
Cinquefoil (Five Finger)	Fire	♃
Clary Sage	Earth	☿
Clover	Air	☿
Cloves	Fire	☉
Evergreen	Fire	☉
Galangel	Fire	♂
Ginger	Fire	♂
Grape	Water	☽
Heliotrope	Fire	☉
High John the Conqueror	Fire	♂
Hollyberry	Fire	♂
Honey	Earth	☉
Honeysuckle	Fire	☉
Hyssop	Fire	♃
Jasmine	Water	☽
Mandrake	Fire	☿
Marigold	Fire	☉
Marjoram	Air	☿
Morning Glory	Earth	♄
Myrrh	Fire	☉
Nutmeg	Fire	V
Orange	Fire	☉
Patchouli	Earth	♄
Pikaki	Water	♀
Pine	Fire	♂
Pineapple	Fire	♂
Sesame	Fire	☉
Spearmint	Air	♀
Tulip	Earth	♀
Verbena	Earth	♀
Vervain	Earth	♀
Vetivert	Earth	♀

RETENTION

Agrimony	Fire	♃
Caraway	Air	☿
Clary Sage	Earth	☿
Coriander	Fire	♂
Dogwood	Air	♀
Honeysuckle	Fire	♂
Ivy	Earth	♄
Juniper	Fire	☉
Lavender	Air	☿
Rose	Air	♀
Sage	Air	♃

STRENGTH OF WILL

Allspice	Earth	♀

SUCCESS

Angelica	Fire	☉
Basil	Fire	♂
Bergamot	Fire	☉
Cedar (Cedarwood)	Fire	♃
Lemon Verbena	Air	♀
Mistletoe	Fire	☉
Musk	Earth	♀
Mustard	Fire	♂
Myrrh	Fire	☉
Orange Blossom	Fire	☉
Vervain	Earth	♀

TRANSFORMATION

Bay	Fire	☉
Hollyberry	Fire	♂
Myrrh	Fire	☉
Peppermint	Fire	☿
Rose	Air	♀
Rosemary	Fire	☉
Spearmint	Air	♀
Vervain	Earth	♀
Violet	Water	♀
Wormwood	Fire	♂

WEALTH

Agrimony	Fire	♃
Almond	Air	♀
Basil	Fire	♂
Bayberry	Earth	☿
Bergamot	Fire	☉
Bindweed	Earth	♄
Cedar (Cedarwood)	Fire	♃
Chamomile	Water	☽
Cinquefoil (Five Finger)	Fire	♃
Clary Sage	Earth	☿
Honeysuckle	Fire	♂
Hyssop	Fire	♃
Jasmine	Water	☽
Morning Glory	Earth	♄

WELL-BEING

Bayberry	Earth	☿

Blessing and Consecration

ANNOINTING

Acacia	Fire	☉
Hyssop	Earth	☉

Lily of the Valley	Air	☿
Spikenard	Earth	♄

ATTUNEMENT

Sweetgrass	Air	♀

BLESSING

Carnation	Fire	☉
Rose Geranium	Fire	♂

CALLING SPIRITS

Sweetgrass	Air	♀

CONSECRATION

Asafoetida	Earth	♄
Basil	Fire	♂
Bay	Fire	☉
Burdock	Earth	♀
Cedar (Cedarwood)	Fire	♃
Cinquefoil (Five Finger)	Fire	♃
Copal	Fire	♃
Eucalyptus	Earth	♄
Galangel	Fire	♂
Hyssop	Fire	♃
Mistletoe	Fire	☉
Musk	Earth	♀
Myrrh	Fire	☉
Peppermint	Fire	☿
Rose	Air	♀
Rose Geranium	Fire	♂
Rosemary	Fire	☉
Rue	Fire	♂
Sage	Air	♃
Spearmint	Air	♀
Thyme	Air	♀
Vervain	Earth	♀

DISPEL NEGATIVITY

Cloves	Fire	☉
Cumin	Fire	♂
Rue	Fire	♂
Spanish Moss	Earth	♄

EMPOWER

Redwood	Earth	⊗

HARMONY AND BALANCE

Acacia	Fire	☉
Althea	Earth	♀
Anise	Air	☿
Basil	Fire	♂
Bay	Fire	☉
Bayberry	Earth	☿
Benzoin	Air	♀
Calamus	Earth	♀
Chamomile	Water	☽
Cherry Blossom	Water	♀
Cinquefoil (Five Finger)	Fire	♃
Clary Sage	Earth	☿
Crab Apple	Air	☿
Geranium	Water	♀
Hibiscus	Water	☽
Honey	Earth	☉
Lavender	Air	☿
Lilac	Water	♀
Marjoram	Air	☿
Myrrh	Fire	☉
Orange	Fire	☉
Orchid	Water	♀
Pennyroyal	Air	♀
Poppy	Water	☽
Redwood	Earth	?
Rose	Air	♀
Sage	Air	♃

Sandalwood	Water	☽
Spikenard	Earth	♄
Valerian	Earth	☿
Ylang-Ylang	Water	♀

HOUSE BLESSING

Bayberry	Earth	☿

INCREASE POWER OF SPELLS

Acacia	Fire	☉
Cinquefoil (Five Finger)	Fire	♃
Copal	Fire	♃
Damiana	Earth	♀
Lemon	Water	☽
Menthol	Fire	♂
Musk	Earth	♀
Patchouli	Earth	♄
Vetivert	Earth	♀

MAGNETIC TO HIGHER VIBRATIONS

Ylang-Ylang	Water	♀
Zula-Zula	Air	♃

OVERCOME OPPOSITION

Asafoetida	Earth	♄
Bay	Fire	☉
Clover	Air	☿
Valerian	Earth	☿
Wormwood	Fire	♂

PURIFICATION

Anise	Air	♃
Azalea	Air	☿
Bay	Fire	☉
Benzoin	Air	♀
Birch	Water	♀
Chamomile	Water	☽

Citronella	Air	☉
Cloves	Fire	☉
Evergreen	Fire	☉
Frankincense	Fire	☉
Hyssop	Fire	♃
Juniper	Fire	☉
Lemon	Water	☽
Lemon-Lime	Water	☽
Mimosa	Water	♄
Peppermint	Fire	☿
Rosemary	Fire	☉
Sage	Air	♃
Thyme	Air	♀
Verbena	Earth	♀

Well-being

Bayberry	Earth	☿

Cleansing, Banishing, and Binding

Banishing

Cumin	Fire	♂
Dragon's Blood	Fire	♀
Eucalyptus	Earth	♄
Frankincense	Fire	☉
Heliotrope	Fire	☉
Lilac	Water	♀
Mint	Air	☿
Mistletoe	Fire	☉
Olibanum (Frankincense)	Fire	☉
Peach	Water	♀
Peony	Fire	☉
Pine	Fire	♂
Rue	Fire	♂

Binding

Ivy	Earth	♄
Orris	Earth	♀

Cleansing

Pine	Fire	♂
Sage	Air	♃

Dispel Negativity

Cloves	Fire	☉
Cumin	Fire	♂
Heliotrope	Fire	☉
Rue	Fire	♂
Spanish Moss	Earth	♄

Endings

Asafoetida	Earth	♄
Bay	Fire	☉
Camphor	Water	☽
Menthol	Fire	♂
Myrrh	Fire	☉
Pennyroyal	Air	♀
Rosemary	Fire	☉

Exorcism

Angelica	Fire	☉
Asafoetida	Earth	♄
Basil	Fire	♂
Bay	Fire	☉
Benzoin	Air	♀
Burdock	Earth	♀
Copal	Fire	♃
Heliotrope	Fire	☉
Menthol	Fire	♂
Mustard	Fire	♂
Myrrh	Fire	☉
Oakmoss	Water	☽
Orris	Earth	♀
Patchouli	Earth	♄
Rose Geranium	Fire	♂
Safflower	Fire	☉
Saffron	Fire	☉
Valerian	Earth	☿
Yerba Santa	Earth	♄

Hex-/Spell-Breaking

Angelica	Fire	☉
Asafoetida	Earth	♄
Basil	Fire	♂
Bay	Fire	☉
Benzoin	Air	♀
Burdock	Earth	♀
Cinquefoil (Five Finger)	Fire	♃
Cloves	Fire	☉
Copal	Fire	♃
Galangel	Fire	♂
Geranium	Water	♀
Lemon Verbena	Air	♀
Menthol	Fire	♂
Mustard	Fire	♂
Myrrh	Fire	☉
Oakmoss	Water	☽
Obeah	Fire	♃
Orris	Earth	♀
Patchouli	Earth	♄
Rose Geranium	Fire	♂
Rosemary	Fire	☉
Rue	Fire	♂
Safflower	Fire	☉
Saffron	Fire	☉
Valerian	Earth	☿
Verbena	Earth	♀
Vetivert	Earth	♀
Wintergreen	Earth	☿
Wormwood	Fire	♂
Yerba Santa	Earth	♄

Increase Power of Spells

Acacia	Fire	☉
Cinquefoil (Five Finger)	Fire	♃
Copal	Fire	♃
Damiana	Earth	♀
Lemon	Water	☽
Menthol	Fire	♂
Musk	Earth	♀
Patchouli	Earth	♄
Vetivert	Earth	♀

Overcome Opposition

Asafoetida	Earth	♄
Bay	Fire	☉
Clover	Air	☿
Valerian	Earth	☿
Wormwood	Fire	♂

Power

Dragon's Blood	Fire	♀
Ginger	Fire	♂
Hemlock	Water	♄
Mandrake	Fire	☿
Obeah	Fire	♃
Van-Van	Earth	♀

Protection

Acacia	Fire	☉
Agrimony	Fire	♃
Anemone	Fire	♂
Angelica	Fire	☉
Anise	Air	☿
Asafoetida	Earth	♄
Balm of Gilead	Fire	♃
Bay	Fire	☉
Bay	Fire	☉
Benzoin	Air	♀
Bindweed	Earth	♄
Birch	Water	♀
Burdock	Earth	♀
Carnation	Fire	☉
Cassia (Cinnamon)	Fire	☉
Clover	Air	☿
Cloves	Fire	☉
Coconut	Water	☽
Copal	Fire	♃
Cranberry	Fire	☉
Cumin	Fire	♂
Cyclamen	Water	♀
Cypress	Earth	♄
Dragon's Blood	Fire	♀
Eucalyptus	Earth	♄
Evergreen	Fire	☉
Frankincense	Fire	☉
Galangel	Fire	♂
Geranium	Water	♀
Grapefruit	Air	☉
Heather	Water	♀
High John the Conqueror	Fire	♂
Hollyberry	Fire	♂
Honeysuckle	Fire	♂
Hyssop	Fire	♃
Juniper	Fire	☉
Lavender	Air	☿
Lilac	Water	♀
Linden	Air	♃
Lotus	Water	☽
Mandrake	Fire	☿
Marjoram	Air	☿
Mimosa	Water	♄
Mint	Air	☿
Morning Glory	Earth	♄
Mugwort	Air	♀
Mustard	Fire	♂
Myrrh	Fire	☉
Obeah	Fire	♃
Olibanum (Frankincense)	Fire	☉
Orris	Earth	♀
Papaya	Water	♀
Patchouli	Earth	♄
Pennyroyal	Air	♀
Pine	Fire	♂
Primrose	Air	♀
Raspberry	Water	☽
Rose Geranium	Fire	♂
Rose, Yellow	Air	♀
Rosemary	Fire	☉
Sage	Air	♃
Sandalwood	Water	☽
Sandalwood, Red	Water	☽
Spanish Moss	Earth	♄
Spearmint	Air	♀
Spruce	Earth	♄
Tangerine	Fire	☉
Tuberose	Fire	☉
Tulip	Earth	♀
Verbena	Earth	♀
Vervain	Earth	♀
Violet	Water	♀
Water Lily	Water	☽
Wintergreen	Earth	☿
Wisteria	Air	♀
Wormwood	Fire	♂
Yerba Santa	Earth	♄
Yula	Water	♆
Cinquefoil (Five Finger)	Fire	♃

Protection—Defense

Tangerine	Fire	☉

PROTECTION—PSYCHIC

Amber	Water	♀
Angelica	Fire	☉
Asafoetida	Earth	W
Basil	Fire	♂
Bay	Fire	☉
Benzoin	Air	♀
Bergamot	Fire	☉
Cinquefoil (Five Finger)	Fire	♃
Cloves	Fire	☉
Cumin	Fire	♂
Galangel	Fire	♂
High John the Conqueror	Fire	♂
Hyssop	Fire	♃
Lemon Verbena	Air	♀
Mandrake	Fire	☿
Marjoram	Air	☿
Mistletoe	Fire	☉
Mugwort	Air	♀
Myrrh	Fire	☉
Patchouli	Earth	♄
Peach	Water	♀
Peony	Fire	☉
Rosewood	Water	☉
Rue	Fire	♂
Spikenard	Earth	♄
Spruce	Earth	♄
Valerian	Earth	☿
Vetivert	Earth	♀

PROTECTION—THEFT

Caraway	Air	☿
Dogwood	Air	♀
Honeysuckle	Fire	♂
Ivy	Earth	♄
Juniper	Fire	☉
Mugwort	Air	♀
Rosemary	Fire	☉

PURIFICATION

Anise	Air	♃
Azalea	Air	☿
Bay	Fire	☉
Benzoin	Air	♀
Birch	Water	♀
Chamomile	Water	☽
Citronella	Air	☉
Cloves	Fire	☉
Evergreen	Fire	☉
Frankincense	Fire	☉
Hyssop	Fire	♃
Juniper	Fire	☉
Lemon	Water	☽
Lemon-Lime	Water	☽
Mimosa	Water	♄
Peppermint	Fire	☿
Rosemary	Fire	☉
Sage	Air	♃
Thyme	Air	♀
Verbena	Earth	♀

RELEASE

Asafoetida	Earth	♄
Bay	Fire	☉
Camphor	Water	☽
Menthol	Fire	♂
Pennyroyal	Air	♀
Peppermint	Fire	☿
Rosemary	Fire	☉
Water Lily	Water	☽

RELEASE INNER NEGATIVITY

Angelica	Fire	☉

SECRETS

Agrimony	Fire	♃
Caraway	Air	☿
Clary Sage	Earth	☿
Coriander	Fire	♂
Dogwood	Air	♀
Honeysuckle	Fire	♂
Ivy	Earth	♄
Juniper	Fire	☉
Juniper	Fire	☉
Lavender	Air	☿
Rose	Air	♀
Sage	Air	♃

Grounding and Centering

CENTERING

Juniper	Fire	☉

CENTERS EMOTIONS

Tuberose	Fire	♂

CLARITY

Azalea	Air	☿
Balsam, Fir	Air	☿
Camphor	Water	☽
Citrus	Air	☉
Evergreen	Fire	☉
Grape	Water	☽
Hyssop	Fire	♃
Lemon	Water	☽
Lemon-Lime	Water	☽
Lilac	Water	♀
Magnolia	Earth	♀
Mint	Air	☿
Peppermint	Fire	☿
Raspberry	Water	☽

Spearmint	Water	♀
Tangerine	Fire	☉
Van-Van	Earth	♀

COMFORT

Cypress	Earth	♄
Evergreen	Fire	☉

COOLING

Birch	Water	♀

FOCUS AND CLARITY

Musk	Earth	♀
Persimmon	Water	♀

GROUNDING

Oakmoss	Earth	☿
Patchouli	Earth	♃
Vetivert	Earth	♀

HARMONY AND BALANCE

Anise	Air	♃
Benzoin	Air	☉
Cherry Blossom	Water	♀
Geranium	Water	♀
Honey	Earth	☉
Lavender	Air	☿
Lilac	Water	♀
Myrrh	Water	☽
Orange	Fire	☉
Orchid	Water	♀
Redwood	Earth	⊗
Sage	Air	♃
Sandalwood	Water	☽
Spikenard	Water	♀
Ylang-Ylang	Water	♀

INNER PEACE

Apple Blossom	Water	♀
Coconut	Water	☽
Rose, White	Water	♀

REFRESHING

Lemon Grass	Air	☿

RESTORATIVE

Marjoram	Air	☿
Myrrh	Air	☿

STRENGTHEN SPIRIT

Ylang-Ylang	Water	♀

WISDOM

Almond	Air	☿
Redwood	Earth	⊗
Sage	Air	♃

Healing, Calming, and Restorative

ANTIDEPRESSANT

Lemon-Lime	Water	☽
Lime	Water	♀
Linden	Air	♃
Olibanum (Frankincense)	Fire	☉
Orange Blossom	Fire	☉
Peppermint	Fire	☿
Tangerine	Fire	☉

BALANCING

Crab Apple	Air	☿

CALMING

Azalea	Air	☿
Benzoin	Air	♀
Birch	Water	♀
Chamomile	Water	☽
Cranberry	Fire	☉
Evergreen	Fire	☉
Geranium	Water	♀
Heliotrope	Fire	☉

Honey	Earth	☉
Honeysuckle	Fire	☉
Lavender	Air	☿
Lemon	Water	☽
Lemon-Lime	Water	☽
Narcissus	Water	X
Nutmeg	Fire	♃
Orange Blossom	Fire	☉
Sandalwood Parvati	Water	☽
Tangerine	Fire	☉
Vanilla	Water	♀
Verbena	Earth	♀
Ylang-Ylang	Water	♀

CENTERING

Juniper	Fire	☉
Lavender	Air	☿
Tuberose	Fire	♂

COMFORT

Cypress	Earth	♄
Evergreen	Fire	☉

CONNECTION TO HIGHER ENERGIES

Redwood	Earth	⊗
Rosewood	Water	☉
Yula	Water	♆
Narcissus	Water	X
Peach	Water	♀

COOLING

Birch	Water	♀

DISPEL NEGATIVITY

Cloves	Fire	☉
Cumin	Fire	♂
Rue	Fire	♂
Spanish Moss	Earth	♄

HARMONY AND BALANCE

Acacia	Fire	☉
Althea	Earth	♀
Anise	Air	☿
Basil	Fire	♂
Bay	Fire	☉
Bayberry	Earth	☿
Benzoin	Air	♀
Calamus	Earth	♀
Chamomile	Water	☽
Cherry Blossom	Water	♀
Cinquefoil (Five Finger)	Fire	♃
Clary Sage	Earth	☿
Geranium	Water	♀
Hibiscus	Water	☽
Honey	Earth	☉
Lavender	Air	☿
Lilac	Water	♀
Marjoram	Air	☿
Myrrh	Fire	☉
Orange	Fire	☉
Orchid	Water	♀
Pennyroyal	Air	♀
Poppy	Water	☽
Redwood	Earth	⊗
Rose	Air	♀
Sage	Air	♃
Sandalwood	Water	☽
Spikenard	Earth	♄
Valerian	Earth	☿
Ylang-Ylang	Water	♀

HEALING

Anemone	Fire	♂
Bay	Fire	☉
Citrus	Air	☉
Cranberry	Fire	☉
Eucalyptus	Earth	♄
Evergreen	Fire	☉
Ginger	Fire	♂
Ginger Blossom	Fire	♂
Grapefruit	Air	☉
Peppermint	Fire	☿
Persimmon	Water	♀
Rue	Fire	♂
Thyme	Air	♀
Violet	Water	♀
Wintergreen	Earth	☿

HEALING—VITALITY

Ginseng	Fire	♂

HEALTH

Spikenard	Earth	♄

HIGHER VIBRATIONS

Dove's Blood	Water	♀

INNER BEAUTY

Orchid	Water	♀

INNER PEACE

Coconut	Water	☽
Rose, White	Air	♀

INNER RADIANCE

Ginseng	Fire	♂

NEW AWARENESS

Freesia	Air	♀

NEW BEGINNINGS

Freesia	Air	♀

OPENING TO HIGHER VIBRATIONS

Aloes Wood

PEACE

Acacia	Fire	☉
Althea	Earth	♀
Basil	Fire	♂
Bay	Fire	☉
Benzoin	Air	♀
Calamus	Earth	♀
Catnip	Air	♀
Chamomile	Water	☽
Cherry Blossom	Water	♀
Gardenia	Water	☽
Lavender	Air	☿
Lilac	Water	♀
Marjoram	Air	☿
Passion Flower	Water	♀
Pennyroyal	Air	♀
Poppy	Water	☽
Rose	Air	♀
Rose, Yellow	Air	♀
Rosewood	Water	☉
Sage	Air	♃
Valerian	Earth	☿
Verbena	Earth	♀
Violet	Water	♀
Ylang-Ylang	Water	♀

PEACE OF MIND

Apple Blossom	Water	♀
Benzoin	Air	♀
Caraway	Air	☿
Honeysuckle	Fire	♂
Lilac	Water	♀
Patchouli	Earth	♄
Rose	Air	♀

REFRESHING

Lemongrass	Air	☿

REGENERATION

Pine	Fire	♂
Vetivert	Earth	♀
Snowdrops	Air	☿

RELAXING

Honeysuckle	Fire	☉
Lotus	Water	☽
Marjoram	Air	☿
Orange	Fire	☉
Orange Blossom	Fire	☉
Vanilla	Water	♀
Ylang-Ylang	Water	♀

RELEASE

Asafoetida	Earth	♄
Bay	Fire	Q
Camphor	Water	☽
Menthol	Fire	♂
Pennyroyal	Air	♀
Peppermint	Fire	☿
Rosemary	Fire	☉
Water Lily	Water	☽

RELEASE INNER NEGATIVITY

Angelica	Fire	☉

RENEWAL

Angelica	Fire	☉
Ginseng	Fire	♂
Marigold	Fire	☉
Mistletoe	Fire	☉
Peppermint	Fire	☿
Snowdrops	Air	☿
Spearmint	Air	♀
Water Lily	Water	☽

REST

Catnip	Air	♀
Jasmine	Water	☽
Linden	Air	♃
Mugwort	Air	♀

RESTORATIVE

Marjoram	Air	☿
Myrrh	Fire	☉

REUNITING

Pineapple	Fire	♂
Violet	Water	♀

SOOTHES WORRIES

Mimosa	Water	♄

STIMULANT—HEALING

Carnation	Fire	☉

TRANSFORMATION

Bay	Fire	☉
Hollyberry	Fire	♂
Myrrh	Fire	☉
Peppermint	Fire	☿
Rose	Air	♀
Rosemary	Fire	☉
Spearmint	Air	♀
Vervain	Earth	♀
Violet	Water	♀
Wormwood	Fire	♂

UPLIFTING

Apple Blossom	Water	♀
Basil	Fire	♂
Cassia (Cinnamon)	Fire	☉
Clover	Air	☿
Crab Apple	Air	☿
Cranberry	Fire	☉
Dittany	Earth	♀
Frankincense	Fire	☉
Geranium	Water	♀
Grapefruit	Air	☉
Jasmine	Water	☽
Lemongrass	Air	☿
Lemon Verbena	Air	♀
Lily of the Valley	Air	☿
Marigold	Fire	☉
Marjoram	Air	☿
Mimosa	Water	♄
Myrrh	Fire	☉
Peppermint	Fire	☿
Rose Geranium	Fire	♂
Rosemary	Fire	☉
Rosemary	Fire	☉
Sesame	Fire	☉
Spearmint	Air	♀

WELL-BEING

Bayberry	Earth	☿

Intuition, Divination, and Psychic Development

ASTRAL PROJECTION

Hemlock	Water	♄

ATTUNEMENT

Sweetgrass	Air	♀

BALANCING

Crab Apple	Air	☿

CALLING SPIRITS

Sweetgrass	Air	♀

CENTERING

Juniper	Fire	☉
Lavender	Air	☿

CENTERS EMOTIONS

Tuberose	Fire	♂

CLAIRVOYANCE

Althea	Earth	♀
Anise	Air	☿
Basil	Fire	♂
Bay	Fire	☉
Cedar (Cedarwood)	Fire	♃
Cinquefoil (Five Finger)	Fire	♃
Clary Sage	Earth	☿
Coriander	Fire	♂
Dittany	Earth	♀
Hibiscus	Water	☽
Honeysuckle	Fire	♂
Ivy	Earth	♄
Lavender	Air	☿
Lilac	Water	♀
Mugwort	Air	♀
Oakmoss	Water	☽
Patchouli	Earth	♄
Poppy	Water	☽
Rose	Air	♀
Thyme	Air	♀
Wormwood	Fire	♂

CONCENTRATION

Orchid	Water	♀
Verbena	Earth	♀

CONNECTION TO HIGHER ENERGIES

Redwood	Earth	⊗
Rosewood	Water	☉
Yula	Water	Y

CONNECTION TO OTHER PLANES

Narcissus	Water	♅

CONNECTION WITH HIGHER SPIRITS

Peach	Water	♀

CONTACT OTHER PLANES

Acacia	Fire	☉
Althea	Earth	♀
Angelica	Fire	☉
Anise	Air	☿
Copal	Fire	♃
Dittany	Earth	♀
Hibiscus	Water	☽
Mistletoe	Fire	☉
Oakmoss	Water	☽
Patchouli	Earth	♄
Rose	Air	♀
Thyme	Air	♀
Wisteria	Air	♀
Wormwood	Fire	♂

CONTROL OF SPIRITUAL ENERGIES

Mandrake	Fire	☿

DIVINATION

Althea	Earth	♀
Anise	Air	☿
Basil	Fire	♂
Bay	Fire	☉
Camphor	Water	☽
Cedar (Cedarwood)	Fire	♃
Cinquefoil (Five Finger)	Fire	♃
Clary Sage	Earth	☿
Coriander	Fire	♂
Dittany	Earth	♀
Green Apple	Water	♀
Hibiscus	Water	☽
Ivy	Earth	♄
Lavender	Air	☿
Lilac	Water	♀
Marigold	Fire	☉
Mugwort	Air	♀
Narcissus	Water	♅
Oakmoss	Water	☽
Orris	Earth	♀
Patchouli	Earth	♄
Poppy	Water	☽
Rose	Air	♀
Rose, Yellow	Air	♀
Sage	Air	♃
Thyme	Air	♀
Wormwood	Fire	♂

DIVINE INTERVENTION

Angelica	Fire	☉
Galangel	Fire	♂
Wisteria	Air	♀
Wormwood	Fire	♂

DREAMS

Catnip	Air	♀
Chamomile	Water	☽
Jasmine	Water	☽
Linden	Air	♃
Mimosa	Water	♄
Mugwort	Air	♀
Nutmeg	Fire	♃
Opium	Water	♆
Poppy	Water	☽

Dreams—Prophetic

Cinquefoil (Five Finger)	Fire	♃
Hollyberry	Fire	♂
Opium	Water	Y
Poppy	Water	☽

Higher Vibrations

Dove's Blood	Water	♀

Increase Power of Spells

Acacia	Fire	☉
Cinquefoil (Five Finger)	Fire	♃
Copal	Fire	♃
Damiana	Earth	♀
Lemon	Water	☽
Menthol	Fire	♂
Musk	Earth	♀
Patchouli	Earth	♄
Vetivert	Earth	♀

Intuition

Hollyberry	Fire	♂
Papaya	Water	♀
Poppy	Water	☽

Magnetic to Higher Vibrations

Ylang-Ylang	Water	♀
Zula-Zula	Air	♃

Manifestation

Oakmoss	Water	☽

Meditation

Acacia	Fire	☉
Chamomile	Water	☽
Cinquefoil (Five Finger)	Fire	♃
Copal	Fire	♃
Dittany	Earth	♀
Frankincense	Fire	☉
Olibanum (Frankincense)	Fire	☉
Rosemary	Fire	☉

Mental Openness

Apricot	Water	♀

Opening to Higher Vibrations

Aloes Wood	Water	☽

Protection—Psychic

Amber	Water	♀
Angelica	Fire	☉
Asafoetida	Earth	♄
Basil	Fire	♂
Bay	Fire	☉
Benzoin	Air	♀
Bergamot	Fire	☉
Cinquefoil (Five Finger)	Fire	♃
Cloves	Fire	☉
Galangel	Fire	♂
Hyssop	Fire	♃
Lemon Verbena	Air	♀
Mandrake	Fire	☿
Marjoram	Air	☿
Mugwort	Air	♀
Myrrh	Fire	☉
Patchouli	Earth	♄
Rosewood	Water	☉
Rue	Fire	♂
Spikenard	Earth	♄
Spruce	Earth	♄
Valerian	Earth	☿
Vetivert	Earth	♀

Psychic Development and Growth

Acacia	Fire	☉
Althea	Earth	♀
Anise	Air	☿
Basil	Fire	♂
Bay	Fire	☉
Clary Sage	Earth	☿
Cloves	Fire	☉
Damiana	Earth	♀
Dittany	Earth	♀
Hibiscus	Water	☽
Lavender	Air	☿
Lemon Grass	Air	☿
Marjoram	Air	☿
Menthol	Fire	♂
Mugwort	Air	♀
Peppermint	Fire	☿
Rue	Fire	♂
Safflower	Fire	☉
Saffron	Fire	☉
Sage	Air	♃
Thyme	Air	♀
Wisteria	Air	♀
Wormwood	Fire	♂
Yerba Santa	Earth	♄

Psychic Powers

Acacia	Fire	☉
Cinnamon (Cassia)	Fire	☉
Citrus	Air	☉
Galangel	Fire	♂
Honeysuckle	Fire	☉
Magnolia	Earth	♀
Peppermint	Fire	☿
Sandalwood Parvati	Water	☽

Water Lily	Water	☽
Wormwood	Fire	♂

VISIONS

Dittany	Earth	♀

Lucky Mojo

ATTRACTION

Amber	Water	♀
Bay	Fire	☉
Bergamot	Fire	☉
Sweet Pea	Water	♀

ATTRACTION—MAGNETISM

Orange Blossom	Fire	☉

BLESSING

Carnation	Fire	☉
Rose Geranium	Fire	♂

COMMANDING

Basil	Fire	♂
Calamus	Earth	♀
Camphor	Water	☽
Catnip	Air	♀
Civet	Fire	☉
Galangel	Fire	♂
Marigold	Fire	☉
Menthol	Fire	♂
Musk	Earth	♀
Mustard	Fire	♂
Orris	Earth	♀
Patchouli	Earth	♄
Poppy	Water	☽
Safflower	Fire	☉
Saffron	Fire	☉
Spikenard	Earth	♄
Vetivert	Earth	♀

EMPOWER

Redwood	Earth	⊗

GAIN

Acacia	Fire	☉
Agrimony	Fire	♃
Angelica	Fire	☉
Caraway	Air	☿
Cedar (Cedarwood)	Fire	♃
Cherry	Air	♀
Juniper	Fire	☉
Mistletoe	Fire	☉
Mustard	Fire	♂
Poppy	Water	☽

GAMBLING

Bindweed	Earth	♄
Morning Glory	Earth	♄

GOOD LUCK

Agrimony	Fire	♃
Allspice	Earth	♀
Anise	Air	☿
Bay	Fire	☉
Bayberry	Earth	☿
Bindweed	Earth	♄
Cassia (Cinnamon)	Fire	☉
Chamomile	Water	☽
Cinquefoil (Five Finger)	Fire	♃
Clover	Air	☿
Galangel	Fire	♂
Heather	Water	♀
Honeysuckle	Fire	♂
Linden	Air	♃
Marigold	Fire	☉

Mistletoe	Fire	☉
Morning Glory	Earth	♄
Musk	Earth	♀
Myrrh	Fire	☉
Nutmeg	Fire	♃
Orange	Fire	☉
Peach	Water	♀
Peony	Fire	☉
Peppermint	Fire	☿
Persimmon	Water	♀
Pineapple	Fire	♂
Poppy	Water	☽
Rose	Air	♀
Rose, White	Air	♀
Rosemary	Fire	☉
Strawberry	Water	♀
Vetivert	Earth	♀
Violet	Water	♀
Water Lily	Water	☽

GROUNDING

Oakmoss	Water	☽
Vetivert	Earth	♀

INCREASE POWER OF SPELLS

Acacia	Fire	☉
Cinquefoil (Five Finger)	Fire	♃
Copal	Fire	♃
Damiana	Earth	♀
Lemon	Water	☽
Menthol	Fire	♂
Musk	Earth	♀
Patchouli	Earth	♄
Vetivert	Earth	♀

MANIFESTATION

Oakmoss	Water	☽

Magical Oils by Moonlight

MATERIAL OBJECTS

Agrimony	Fire	♃
Almond	Air	♀
Basil	Fire	♂
Bayberry	Earth	☿
Bergamot	Fire	☉
Bindweed	Earth	♄
Cedar (Cedarwood)	Fire	♃
Chamomile	Water	☽
Cinquefoil (Five Finger)	Fire	♃
Clary Sage	Earth	☿
Honeysuckle	Fire	♂
Hyssop	Fire	♃
Jasmine	Water	☽
Mandrake	Fire	☿
Morning Glory	Earth	♄
Myrrh	Fire	☉
Orange	Fire	☉
Peppermint	Fire	☿
Poppy	Water	☽
Vervain	Earth	♀

OVERCOME OPPOSITION

Asafoetida	Earth	♄
Bay	Fire	☉
Clover	Air	☿
Valerian	Earth	☿
Wormwood	Fire	♂

POWER

Dragon's Blood	Fire	♀
Ginger	Fire	♂
Hemlock	Water	♄
Mandrake	Fire	☿
Obeah	Fire	♃
Van-Van	Earth	♀

RETENTION

Agrimony	Fire	♃
Caraway	Air	☿
Clary Sage	Earth	☿
Coriander	Fire	♂
Dogwood	Air	♀
Honeysuckle	Fire	♂
Ivy	Earth	♄
Juniper	Fire	☉
Lavender	Air	☿
Rose	Air	♀
Sage	Air	♃
Pineapple	Fire	♂
Violet	Water	♀

SUCCESS

Angelica	Fire	☉
Basil	Fire	♂
Bergamot	Fire	☉
Cedar (Cedarwood)	Fire	♃
Lemon Verbena	Air	♀
Mistletoe	Fire	☉
Musk	Earth	♀
Mustard	Fire	♂
Myrrh	Fire	☉
Orange Blossom	Fire	☉
Vervain	Earth	♀

WISHES

Peach	Water	♀
Sandalwood Parvati	Water	☽
Violet	Water	♀
Walnut	Fire	☉
Wisteria	Air	♀

Mental Clarity and Awareness

ANTIDEPRESSANT

Lemon-Lime	Water	☽
Lime	Water	♀
Linden	Air	♃
Olibanum (Frankincense)	Fire	☉
Orange Blossom	Fire	☉
Peppermint	Fire	☿
Tangerine	Fire	☉

ATTUNEMENT

Sweetgrass	Air	♀

CENTERING

Juniper	Fire	☉
Lavender	Air	☿
Tuberose	Fire	♂

CHAKRA—BROW

Myrrh	Fire	☉

CHAKRA—CROWN

Aloes Wood	Earth	☽
Dragon's Blood	Fire	♀
Lotus	Water	☽
Myrrh	Fire	☉

CHAKRA—THROAT

Violet	Water	♀

CLARITY

Azalea	Air	☿
Balsam, Fir	Air	☿
Camphor	Water	☽
Citrus	Air	☉
Clary Sage	Earth	☿
Evergreen	Fire	☉

Grape	Water	☽
Hyssop	Fire	♃
Lemon	Water	☽
Lemon-Lime	Water	☽
Lilac	Water	♀
Magnolia	Earth	♀
Mint	Air	☿
Peppermint	Fire	☿
Raspberry	Water	☽
Spearmint	Air	♀
Tangerine	Fire	☉
Van-Van	Earth	♀

Concentration

Orchid	Water	♀
Verbena	Earth	♀

Creativity

Apricot	Water	♀
Cassia (Cinnamon)	Fire	☉
Hyssop	Fire	♃
Tangerine	Fire	☉
Vervain	Earth	♀

Focus and Clarity

Persimmon	Water	♀

Grounding

Oakmoss	Water	☽
Vetivert	Earth	♀

Inspiration

Balm of Gilead	Fire	♃
Bay	Fire	☉
Benzoin	Air	♀
Cinquefoil (Five Finger)	Fire	♃
Tangerine	Fire	☉
Vervain	Earth	♀
Wisteria	Air	♀
Angelica	Fire	☉

Knowledge

Angelica	Fire	☉
Balm of Gilead	Fire	♃
Bay	Fire	☉
Benzoin	Air	♀
Cinquefoil (Five Finger)	Fire	♃
Clary Sage	Earth	☿
Vervain	Earth	♀
Wisteria	Air	♀

Memory

Wintergreen	Earth	☿

Memory and Concentration

Bay	Fire	☉
Benzoin	Air	♀
Caraway	Air	☿
Clary Sage	Earth	☿
Honeysuckle	Fire	♂
Lilac	Water	♀
Marigold	Fire	☉
Mint	Air	☿
Rosemary	Fire	☉

Mental Focus

Citrus	Air	☉
Eucalyptus	Earth	♄

Mental Openness

Apricot	Water	♀

Mental Powers

Cloves	Fire	☉
Cypress	Earth	♄
Hyssop	Fire	♃
Lemon	Water	☽
Lily of the Valley	Air	☿
Rosemary	Fire	☉
Spearmint	Air	♀
Vanilla	Water	♀
Van-Van	Earth	♀

Persuasion

Orange Blossom	Fire	☉

Refreshing

Lemon Grass	Air	☿

Release Inner Negativity

Angelica	Fire	☉

Restorative

Marjoram	Air	☿
Myrrh	Fire	☉

Soothes Worries

Mimosa	Water	♄

Stimulant

Eucalyptus	Earth	♄
Lavender	Air	☿
Lemon-Lime	Water	☽
Lime	Water	♀
Linden	Air	♃
Orange	Fire	☉

Uplifting

Apple Blossom	Water	♀
Basil	Fire	♂
Cinnamon (Cassia)	Fire	☉
Clover	Air	☿
Crab Apple	Air	☿
Cranberry	Fire	☉
Dittany	Earth	♀
Frankincense	Fire	☉

Geranium	Water	♀
Grapefruit	Air	☉
Jasmine	Water	☽
Lemon Grass	Air	☿
Lemon Verbena	Air	♀
Lily of the Valley	Air	☿
Marigold	Fire	☉
Marjoram	Air	☿
Mimosa	Water	♄
Myrrh	Fire	☉
Peppermint	Fire	☿
Rose Geranium	Fire	♂
Rosemary	Fire	☉
Sesame	Fire	☉
Spearmint	Air	♀

Well-Being

Bayberry	Earth	☿

Wisdom

Almond	Air	☿
Angelica	Fire	☉
Balm of Gilead	Fire	♃
Bay	Fire	☉
Benzoin	Air	♀
Cinquefoil (Five Finger)	Fire	♃
Clary Sage	Earth	☿
Redwood	Earth	⊗
Rosemary	Fire	☉
Sage	Air	♃
Sandalwood	Water	☽

Personal Empowerment and Attraction

Attraction

Amber	Water	♀
Bay	Fire	☉
Bergamot	Fire	☉
Sweet Pea	Water	♀

Attraction—Customers

Mistletoe	Fire	☉
Peony	Fire	☉

Attraction—Friends and customers

Amber	Water	♀
Citronella	Fire	♃
Linden	Air	♃

Attraction—Love

Linden	Air	♃
Lotus	Water	☽
Orange	Fire	☉

Attraction—Magnetism

Orange Blossom	Fire	☉

Attraction—Opposite Sex

Frangipani	Water	♀

Attunement

Sweetgrass	Air	♀

Balancing

Crab Apple	Air	☿

Centering

Juniper	Fire	☉
Lavender	Air	☿
Tuberose	Fire	♂

Chakra—Union

Hibiscus	Water	☽

Character

Rosemary	Fire	☉
Tuberose	Fire	♂

Confidence

Rose Geranium	Fire	♂
Rosemary	Fire	☉

Connection to Higher Energies

Redwood	Earth	⊗
Rosewood	Water	☉
Yula	Water	♆

Connection to Higher Spirits

Peach	Water	♀

Courage

Coconut	Water	☽
Musk	Earth	♀
Rose Geranium	Fire	♂
Rosemary	Fire	☉
Sweet Pea	Water	♀
Thyme	Air	♀

Determination

Althea	Earth	♀
Chamomile	Water	☽
Honeysuckle	Fire	♂
Wormwood	Fire	♂

Dispel Negativity

Cloves	Fire	☉
Cumin	Fire	♂
Rue	Fire	♂
Spanish Moss	Earth	♄

ELOQUENCE

Citronella	Fire	♃

EMPOWER

Redwood	Earth	⊗

ENERGIZES

Ginger	Fire	♂

ENERGY

Anemone	Fire	♂

FOCUS AND CLARITY

Persimmon	Water	♀

GROUNDING

Oakmoss	Water	☽
Vetivert	Earth	♀

HAPPINESS

Amber	Water	♀
Apple Blossom	Water	♀
Basil	Fire	♂
Cherry Blossom	Water	♀
Dittany	Earth	♀
Hyacinth	Earth	☉
Jasmine	Water	☽
Lemon Verbena	Air	♀
Lily of the Valley	Air	☿
Marigold	Fire	☉
Marjoram	Air	S
Myrrh	Fire	☉
Orange	Fire	☉
Orange, Mandarin	Fire	☉
Peppermint	Fire	☿
Rosemary	Fire	☉
Safflower	Fire	☉
Saffron	Fire	☉
Spearmint	Air	♀
Strawberry	Water	♀
Violet	Water	♀

HARMONY AND BALANCE

Acacia	Fire	☉
Althea	Earth	♀
Anise	Air	☿
Basil	Fire	♂
Bay	Fire	☉
Bayberry	Earth	☿
Benzoin	Air	♀
Calamus	Earth	♀
Chamomile	Water	☽
Cherry Blossom	Water	♀
Cinquefoil (Five Finger)	Fire	♃
Clary Sage	Earth	☿
Geranium	Water	♀
Hibiscus	Water	☽
Honey	Earth	☉
Lavender	Air	☿
Lilac	Water	♀
Marjoram	Air	☿
Myrrh	Fire	☉
Orange	Fire	☉
Orchid	Water	♀
Pennyroyal	Air	♀
Poppy	Water	☽
Redwood	Earth	⊗
Rose	Air	♀
Sage	Air	♃
Sandalwood	Water	☽
Spikenard	Earth	♄
Valerian	Earth	☿
Ylang-Ylang	Water	♀

INCREASE POWER OF SPELLS

Acacia	Fire	☉
Cinquefoil (Five Finger)	Fire	♃
Copal	Fire	♃
Damiana	Earth	♀
Lemon	Water	☽
Menthol	Fire	♂
Musk	Earth	♀
Patchouli	Earth	♄
Vetivert	Earth	♀

INNER BEAUTY

Orchid	Water	♀

INNER PEACE

Coconut	Water	☽
Rose, White	Air	♀

INNER RADIANCE

Ginseng	Fire	♂

INSPIRATION

Balm of Gilead	Fire	♃
Bay	Fire	☉
Benzoin	Air	♀
Cinquefoil (Five Finger)	Fire	♃
Tangerine	Fire	☉
Vervain	Earth	♀
Wisteria	Air	♀
Angelica	Fire	☉

NEW AWARENESS

Freesia	Air	♀

NEW BEGINNINGS

Freesia	Air	♀

OPENING TO HIGHER VIBRATIONS

Aloes Wood		

Optimism

Heliotrope	Fire	☉
Hyacinth	Earth	☉
Lily of the Valley	Air	☿
Persimmon	Water	♀
Raspberry	Water	☽

Overcome Opposition

Asafoetida	Earth	♄
Bay	Fire	☉
Clover	Air	☿
Valerian	Earth	☿
Wormwood	Fire	♂

Persuasion

Orange Blossom	Fire	☉

Power

Dragon's Blood	Fire	♀
Ginger	Fire	♂
Hemlock	Water	♄
Mandrake	Fire	☿
Obeah	Fire	♃
Van-Van	Earth	♀

Self-Esteem

Grapefruit	Air	☉

Soothes Worries

Mimosa	Water	♄

Strength

Amber	Water	♀
Balm of Gilead	Fire	♃
Basil	Fire	♂
Bergamot	Fire	Q
Blue Bonnet	Air	☿
Carnation	Fire	Q
Cedar (Cedarwood)	Fire	♃
Clover	Air	☿
Evergreen	Fire	Q
Frankincense	Fire	Q
Ginger	Fire	♂
Ginseng	Fire	♂
Juniper	Fire	☉
Lavender	Air	☿
Lime	Water	♀
Linden	Air	♃
Mugwort	Air	♀
Musk	Earth	♀
Mustard	Fire	♂
Nutmeg	Fire	♃
Peach	Water	♀
Pennyroyal	Air	♀
Pine	Fire	♂
Rosemary	Fire	☉
Sage	Air	♃
Sassafras	Fire	♃
Spruce	Earth	♄
Sweet Pea	Water	♀
Thyme	Air	♀
Vetivert	Earth	♀
Yerba Santa	Earth	♄

Strength of Will

Allspice	Earth	♀

Strengthen Spirit

Ylang-Ylang	Water	♀

Success

Angelica	Fire	☉
Basil	Fire	♂
Bergamot	Fire	☉
Cedar (Cedarwood)	Fire	♃
Lemon Verbena	Air	♀
Mistletoe	Fire	☉
Musk	Earth	♀
Mustard	Fire	♂
Myrrh	Fire	☉
Orange Blossom	Fire	☉
Vervain	Earth	♀

Transformation

Bay	Fire	☉
Hollyberry	Fire	♂
Myrrh	Fire	☉
Peppermint	Fire	☿
Rose	Air	♀
Rosemary	Fire	☉
Spearmint	Air	♀
Vervain	Earth	♀
Violet	Water	♀
Wormwood	Fire	♂

Well-being

Bayberry	Earth	☿

Appendix B:
Oil Properties Master List

ACACIA   FIRE ☉

Anointing
Contact Other Planes
Gain
Harmony and Balance
Increase Power of Spells
Insure Agreements
  and Contracts
Meditation
Money
Peace
Protection
Psychic Development and
  Growth
Psychic Powers

AGRIMONY   FIRE ♃

Gain
Good Luck
Material Objects
Money
Prosperity/Money
Protection
Retention
Secrets
Wealth

ALLSPICE   EARTH ♀

Chakra—Belly
Compassion
Good Luck
Prosperity/Money

**STRENGTH OF
WILL**   AIR ♀

Almond
Alertness
Compassion
Love
Love—Aphrodisiac
Love—Fertility
Material Objects
Money
Prosperity/Money
Wealth
Wisdom

ALOES WOOD

Chakra—Crown
Opening to Higher
  Vibrations

ALTHEA   EARTH ♀

Clairvoyance
Contact Other Planes
Determination
Divination
Harmony and Balance
Peace
Psychic Development and
  Growth

AMBER   WATER ♀

Attraction
Attraction—
  FriendsandCustomers
Happiness
Love
Past-Life Soul Mate
Protection—Psychic
Strength

AMBERGRIS   AIR ♀

Love
Passion

ANEMONE   FIRE ♂

Energy

Magical Oils by Moonlight

Healing
Protection

ANGELICA   FIRE   ☉

Contact Other Planes
Divine Intervention
Exorcism
Gain
Hex-/Spell-Breaking
Inspiration
Knowledge
Love
Magic
Protection
Protection—Psychic
Release Inner Negativity
Renewal
Success
Wisdom

ANISE   AIR   ☿

Clairvoyance
Contact Other Planes
Divination
Good Luck
Harmony and Balance
Money
Protection
Psychic Development
  and Growth
Purification   ♃

APPLE BLOSSOM   WATER ♀

Happiness
Love
Peace of Mind
Uplifting

APRICOT   WATER ♀

Creativity
Love
Mental Openness

ASAFOETIDA   EARTH   ♄

Consecration
Endings
Exorcism
Hex-/Spell-Breaking
Overcome Opposition
Protection
Protection—Psychic
Release

ASTER   WATER ♀

Love
Love—Unconditional

AZALEA   AIR   ☿

Calming
Clarity
Purification

BALM OF GILEAD   FIRE   ♃

Inspiration
Knowledge
Love
Protection
Strength
Virility
Wisdom

BALSAM, FIR   AIR   ☿

Clarity
Prosperity/Money

BANANA   WATER ♀

Prosperity/Money

BASIL   FIRE   ♂

Clairvoyance
Commanding
Consecration
Divination
Exorcism
Fidelity
Happiness
Harmony and Balance
Hex-/Spell-Breaking
Honesty
Love
Love—Aphrodisiac
Love—Fertility
Material Objects
Money
Passion
Peace
Prosperity/Money
Protection—Psychic
Psychic Development
  and Growth
Strength
Success
Uplifting
Wealth

BAY   FIRE   ☉

Attraction
Clairvoyance
Consecration
Divination
Endings
Exorcism
Good Luck

Harmony and Balance
Healing
Hex-/Spell-Breaking
Inspiration
Knowledge
Love
Love—Aphrodisiac
Magic
Memory and
  Concentration
Money
Overcome Opposition
Peace
Protection
Protection—Psychic
Psychic Development
  and Growth
Purification
Release
Transformation
Wisdom

BAYBERRY   EARTH ♀

Domestic Tranquility
Good Luck
Harmony and Balance
House Blessing Material
Objects
Prosperity/Money
Wealth
Well-Being

BENZOIN   AIR   ♀

Calming
Exorcism
Harmony and Balance
Hex-/Spell-Breaking
Inspiration
Knowledge

Love
Memory and
  Concentration
Peace
Peace of Mind
Prosperity/Money
Protection
Protection—Psychic
Purification
Wisdom

BERGAMOT   FIRE   ☉

Attraction
Love
Love—Aphrodisiac
Material Objects
Money
Prosperity/Money
Protection—Psychic
Sensuality
Strength
Success
Wealth

BINDWEED   EARTH ♄

Gambling
Good Luck
Law
Love
Material Objects
Money
Prosperity/Money
Protection
Wealth

BIRCH   WATER ♀

Calming
Cooling

Protection
Purification   ♀

BLUE BONNET   AIR   ♀

Prosperity/Money
Strength

BURDOCK   EARTH ♀

Compassion
Consecration
Exorcism
Hex-/Spell-Breaking
Love
Protection

CALAMUS   EARTH ♀

Commanding
Harmony and Balance
Love
Love—Aphrodisiac
Peace

CAMELLIA   WATER ☽

Gentleness
Prosperity/Money

CAMPHOR   WATER ☽

Clarity
Commanding
Divination
Endings
Release

CARAWAY   AIR   ♀

Fidelity
Gain
Honesty
Love—Fertility

Memory and
  Concentration
Peace of Mind
Protection—Theft
Retention
Secrets

CARNATION   FIRE ☉
Blessing
Protection
Stimulant—Healing
Strength

CASSIA
(CINNAMON) FIRE ☉
Creativity
Good Luck
Love—Power
Protection
Psychic Powers
Uplifting

CATNIP   AIR ♀
Commanding
Dreams
Peace
Rest
Shape-Changing
Sleep

CEDAR
(CEDARWOOD) FIRE ♃
Clairvoyance
Consecration
Divination
Gain
Material Objects
Prosperity/Money

Strength
Success
Wealth

CHAMOMILE WATER ☽
Beauty
Calming
Determination
Dreams
Gentleness
Good Luck
Harmony and Balance
Material Objects
Meditation
Modesty
Peace
Prosperity/Money
Purification
Wealth

CHERRY   AIR ♀
Gain
Love
Love—Fertility

CHERRY
BLOSSOM WATER ♀
Happiness
Harmony and Balance
Peace

CINNAMON
(CASSIA) FIRE ☉
Creativity
Good Luck
Love—Power
Protection
Psychic Powers
Uplifting

CINQUEFOIL
(FIVE FINGER) FIRE ♃
Clairvoyance
Consecration
Divination
Dreams—Prophetic
Good Luck
Harmony and Balance
Hex-/Spell-Breaking
Increase Power of Spells
Inspiration
Knowledge
Material Objects
Meditation
Prosperity/Money
Protection
Protection—Psychic
Wealth
Wisdom

CITRONELLA FIRE ♃
Attraction—
  Friends and Customers
Eloquence
Purification

CITRUS   AIR ☉
Clarity
Healing
Mental Focus
Psychic Powers

CIVET   FIRE ♀
Chakra—Base
Commanding
Love
Love—Aphrodisiac
Sensuality
Virility

CLARY SAGE   EARTH ☿

Clairvoyance
Clarity
Divination
Harmony and Balance
Knowledge
Material Objects
Memory and
   Concentration
Prosperity/Money
Psychic Development
   and Growth
Retention
Secrets
Wealth
Wisdom

CLOVER   AIR ☿

Good Luck
Love—Fidelity
Overcome Opposition
Prosperity/Money
Protection
Strength
Uplifting

CLOVES   FIRE ☉

Dispel Negativity
Hex-/Spell-Breaking
Love
Mental Powers
Prosperity/Money
Protection
Protection—Psychic
Psychic Development
   and Growth
Purification

COCONUT   WATER ☽

Courage
Inner Peace
Love
Protection

COPAL   FIRE ♃

Consecration
Contact Other Planes
Exorcism
Hex-/Spell-Breaking
Increase Power of Spells
Meditation
Protection

CORIANDER   FIRE ♂

Clairvoyance
Divination
Retention
Secrets

CRAB APPLE   AIR ☿

Balancing
Uplifting

CRANBERRY   FIRE ☉

Calming
Defense
Healing
Protection
Uplifting

CUMIN   FIRE ♂

Banishing
Dispel Negativity
Love—Fidelity
Protection
Protection—
   Reversing

CYCLAMEN   WATER ♀

Chakra—Heart
Passion
Protection

CYPRESS   EARTH ♄

Comfort
Longevity
Mental Powers
Protection

DAMIANA   EARTH ♀

Increase Power of Spells
Love—Aphrodisiac
Psychic Development
   and Growth
Sensuality

DITTANY   EARTH ♀

Clairvoyance
Contact Other Planes
Divination
Happiness
Meditation
Psychic Development
   and Growth
Uplifting
Visions

DOGWOOD   AIR ♀

Fidelity
Honesty
Protection—Theft
Retention
Secrets

DOVE'S BLOOD   WATER ♀

Higher Vibrations
Love

DRAGON'S
BLOOD   FIRE ♀

Banishing
Chakra—Crown
Love
Power
Protection

EUCALYPTUS   EARTH ♄

Banishing
Consecration
Healing
Mental Focus
Protection
Stimulant

EVERGREEN   FIRE ☉

Calming
Clarity
Comforting
Healing
Prosperity/Money
Protection
Purification
Strength

FRANGIPANI
(PLUMERIA)   WATER ♀

Attraction
  (Opposite Sex)
Chakra—Base
Chakra—Heart
Love

FRANKINCENSE   FIRE ☉

Banishing
Meditation

Protection
Purification
Spirituality
Strength
Uplifting

FREESIA   AIR ♀

Chakra—Heart
New Awareness
New Beginnings

GALANGEL   FIRE ♂

Commanding
Consecration
Divine Intervention
Good Luck
Hex-/Spell-Breaking
Law
Money
Passion
Prosperity/Money
Protection
Protection—Psychic
Psychic Powers

GARDENIA   WATER ☽

Chakra—Heart
Love
Peace
Spirituality

GERANIUM   WATER ♀

Calming
Harmony and Balance
Hex-/Spell-Breaking
Love—Fertility
Protection
Uplifting

GINGER   FIRE ♂

Energizes
Healing
Love
Passion
Power
Prosperity/Money
Strength

GINGER
BLOSSOM   FIRE ♂

Chakra—Base
Healing
Love
Passion

GINSENG   FIRE ♂

Healing—Vitality
Inner Radiance
Love
Passion
Renewal
Strength

GRAPE   WATER ☽

Clarity
Love—Fertility
Prosperity/Money

GRAPEFRUIT   AIR ☉

Healing
Protection
Self-Esteem
Uplifting

GREEN APPLE   WATER ♀

Divination

HEATHER   WATER ♀
Good Luck
Protection

HELIOTROPE   FIRE ☉
Banishing
Calming
Optimism
Prosperity/Money

HEMLOCK   WATER ♄
Astral Projection
Power

HIBISCUS   WATER ☽
Chakra—Union
Clairvoyance
Contact Other Planes
Divination
Harmony and Balance
Love
Passion
Psychic Development
   and Growth

**HIGH JOHN THE
CONQUEROR**   FIRE ♂
Love
Prosperity/Money
Protection
Protection—Reversing

HOLLYBERRY   FIRE ♂
Dreams—Prophetic
Intuition
Love
Prosperity/Money
Protection
Transformation

HONEY   EARTH ☉
Calming
Harmony and Balance
Love
Prosperity/Money

HONEYSUCKLE   FIRE
Calming ☉
Clairvoyance ♂
Determination
Fidelity
Good Luck
Material Objects
Memory and
   Concentration
Peace of Mind
Prosperity/Money ☉
Protection ♂
Protection—Theft
Psychic Powers ☉
Relaxing
Retention ♂
Secrets
Wealth

HYACINTH   EARTH☉
Happiness
Love
Optimism

HYSSOP
Anointing   EARTH ☉
Clarity   FIRE ♃
Consecration
Creativity
Material Objects
Mental Powers
Prosperity/Money

Protection
Protection—Psychic
Purification
Wealth

IVY   EARTH ♄
Binding
Clairvoyance
Divination
Fidelity
Honesty
Protection—Theft
Retention
Secrets

JASMINE   WATER ☽
Dreams
Happiness
Love
Love—Aphrodisiac
Love—Fertility
Love—Spiritual
Material Objects
Prosperity/Money
Rest
Sleep
Uplifting
Wealth

JUNIPER   FIRE ☉
Centering
Gain
Love
Protection
Protection—Theft
Purification
Retention
Secrets
Strength

209

Magical Oils by Moonlight

LAVENDER   AIR   ☿

Calming
Centering
Clairvoyance
Divination
Gentleness
Harmony and Balance
Love
Peace
Protection
Psychic Development
   and Growth
Retention
Secrets
Stimulant
Strength

LEMON   WATER ☽

Calming
Clarity
Increase Power of Spells
Love—Friendship
Mental Powers
Purification

LEMON GRASS   AIR   ☿

Fidelity
Honesty
Passion
Psychic Development
   and Growth
Refreshing
Uplifting

LEMON VERBENA   AIR   ♀

Happiness
Hex- /Spell-Breaking

Protection—Psychic
Success
Uplifting

LEMON-LIME   WATER ☽

Antidepressant
Calming
Clarity
Love—Friendship
Purification
Stimulant

LILAC   WATER ♀

Banishing
Clairvoyance
Clarity
Divination
Harmony and Balance
Memory and
   Concentration
Peace
Peace of Mind
Protection

LILY OF THE VALLEY   AIR   ☿

Anointing
Happiness
Mental Powers
Optimism
Uplifting

LIME   WATER ♀

Antidepressant
Love—Fidelity
Love—Friendship
Stimulant
Strength

LINDEN   AIR   ♃

Antidepressant
Attraction—Friends and
   Customers
Attraction—Love
Beauty
Dreams
Good Luck
Protection
Rest
Sleep
Stimulant
Strength

LOTUS   WATER ☽

Attraction—Love
Chakra—Crown
Higher Awareness
Protection
Relaxing
Sensuality
Spirituality

MAGNOLIA   EARTH ♀

Clarity
Love—Fidelity
Psychic Powers
Purity

MANDRAKE   FIRE   ☿

Control of Spiritual
   Energies
Love—Fertility
Material Objects
Power
Prosperity/Money
Protection
Protection—Psychic
Virility

210

MARIGOLD   FIRE ☉

Commanding
Divination
Good Luck
Happiness
Memory and
   Concentration
Prosperity/Money
Renewal
Uplifting

MARJORAM   AIR ☿

Happiness
Harmony and Balance
Peace
Prosperity/Money
Protection
Protection—Psychic
Psychic Development
   and Growth
Relaxing
Restorative
Uplifting

MENTHOL   FIRE ♂

Commanding
Endings
Exorcism
Hex-/Spell-Breaking
Increase Power of Spells
Psychic Development
   and Growth
Release

MIMOSA   WATER ♄

Dreams
Love
Protection

Purification
Soothes Worries
Uplifting

MINT   AIR ☿

Banishing
Clarity
Memory and
   Concentration
Passion
Protection
Travel

MISTLETOE   FIRE ☉

Attraction—Customers
Banishing
Consecration
Contact Other Planes
Gain
Good Luck
Love—Fertility
Protection—Reversing
Renewal
Success
Virility

MORNING GLORY   EARTH ♄

Gambling
Good Luck
Law
Love
Material Objects
Money
Prosperity/Money
Protection
Wealth

MUGWORT   AIR ♀

Clairvoyance
Divination
Dreams
Love—Aphrodisiac
Protection
Protection—Psychic
Protection—Theft
Psychic Development
   and Growth
Rest
Sleep
Strength

MUSK   EARTH ♀

Commanding
Consecration
Courage
Good Luck
Increase Power of Spells
Love—Aphrodisiac
Love—Passion
Sensuality
Strength
Success
Virility

MUSTARD   FIRE ♂

Commanding
Exorcism
Gain
Hex-/Spell-Breaking
Love—Fertility
Passion
Protection
Strength
Success
Virility

Magical Oils by Moonlight

MYRRH — FIRE ☉

Chakra—Brow
Chakra—Crown
Compassion
Consecration
Endings
Exorcism
Good Luck
Happiness
Harmony and Balance
Hex-/Spell-Breaking
Material Objects
Prosperity/Money
Protection
Protection—Psychic
Restorative
Success
Transformation
Uplifting
Virility

NARCISSUS — WATER ♅

Calming
Connection to Other Planes
Divination

NUTMEG — FIRE ♃

Calming
Dreams
Good Luck
Love—Fidelity
Prosperity/Money
Strength

OAKMOSS — WATER ☽

Clairvoyance
Contact Other Planes
Divination
Exorcism
Grounding
Hex-/Spell-Breaking
Manifestation

OBEAH — FIRE ♃

Hex-/Spell-Breaking
Power
Protection

OLIBANUM (FRANKINCENSE) — FIRE ☉

Antidepressant
Banishing
Meditation
Protection
Spirituality

OPIUM — WATER ♆

Dreams
Dreams—Prophetic
Love—Aphrodisiac
Sleep

ORANGE — FIRE ☉

Attraction—Love
Beauty
Good Luck
Happiness
Harmony and Balance
Love
Love—Fertility Material Objects
Prosperity/Money
Relaxing
Sensuality
Stimulant

ORANGE BLOSSOM — FIRE ☉

Antidepressant
Attraction (Magnetism)
Calming
Chakra—Belly
Chakra—Heart
Love
Persuasion
Relaxing
Success

ORANGE, MANDARIN — FIRE ☉

Happiness

ORCHID — WATER ♀

Concentration
Harmony and Balance
Inner Beauty
Love

ORRIS — EARTH ♀

Binding
Commanding
Divination
Exorcism
Hex-/Spell-Breaking
Love—Binding
Protection

PAPAYA — WATER ♀

Intuition
Love
Protection

212

PASSION
FLOWER   WATER ♀

Friendship
Peace

PATCHOULI   EARTH ♄

Clairvoyance
Commanding
Contact Other Planes
Divination
Exorcism
Grounding
Hex- /Spell-Breaking
Increase Power of Spells
Love—Aphrodisiac
Love—Fertility
Passion
Peace of Mind
Prosperity/Money
Protection
Protection—Psychic

PEACH   WATER ♀

Banishing
Connection with Higher
  Spirits
Good Luck
Love—Fertility
Protection—Reversing
Strength
Wishes

PENNYROYAL   AIR   ♀

Endings
Harmony and Balance
Peace
Protection
Release
Strength

PEONY   FIRE   ☉

Attraction—Customers
Banishing
Good Luck
Protection—Reversing

PEPPERMINT   FIRE   ☿

Antidepressant
Clarity
Consecration
Good Luck
Happiness
Healing
Material Objects
Psychic Development
  and Growth
Psychic Powers
Purification
Release
Renewal
Transformation
Uplifting

PERSIMMON   WATER ♀

Focus and Clarity
Good Luck
Healing
Optimism

PIKAKI   WATER ♀

Passion
Prosperity/Money

PINE   FIRE   ♂

Banishing
Cleansing
Love—Fertility
Prosperity/Money

Protection
Regeneration
Strength

PINEAPPLE   FIRE   ♂

Good Luck
Prosperity/Money
Reuniting

PLUMERIA
(FRANGIPANI)   WATER ♀

Attraction (Opposite Sex)
Chakra—Base
Chakra—Heart
Love
Passion

POPPY   WATER ☽

Clairvoyance
Commanding
Compassion
Divination
Dreams
Gain
Good Luck
Harmony and Balance
Intuition
Invisibility
Love—Fertility
Material Objects
Peace
Prophetic Dreams
Sleep

PRIMROSE   AIR   ♀

Love
Protection
Spirituality
Truth

213

Magical Oils by Moonlight

RASPBERRY WATER ☽

Clarity
Love
Optimism
Protection

REDWOOD EARTH ⊗

Connection to Higher
  Energies
Empower
Harmony and Balance
Wisdom

ROSE AIR ♀

Beauty
Clairvoyance
Compassion
Consecration
Contact Other Planes
Divination
Good Luck
Harmony and Balance
Love
Peace
Peace of Mind
Retention
Secrets
Transformation

ROSE
GERANIUM FIRE ♂

Blessing
Confidence
Consecration
Courage
Exorcism
Hex-/Spell-Breaking

Love—Passion
Protection
Uplifting

ROSE, RED AIR ♀

Love

ROSE, WHITE AIR ♀

Good Luck
Inner Peace

ROSE, WILD AIR ♀

Love

ROSE, YELLOW AIR ♀

Love
Divination
Peace
Protection

ROSEMARY FIRE ☉

Character
Confidence
Consecration
Courage
Endings
Good Luck
Happiness
Hex-/Spell-Breaking
Love—Fidelity
Love—Passion
Meditation
Memory and
  Concentration
Mental Powers
Protection
Protection—Theft
Purification
Release

Strength
Transformation
Uplifting
Wisdom

ROSEWOOD WATER ☉

Connection to Higher
  Energies
Peace
Protection—Psychic

ROWAN FIRE ☉

Healing
Power
Protection
Inspiration
Success
Resistance to Negative
  Forces

RUE FIRE ♂

Banishing
Compassion
Consecration
Dispel Negativity
Healing
Hex-/Spell-Breaking
Karma
Love
Protection—Psychic
Psychic Development
  and Growth

SAFFLOWER FIRE ☉

Commanding
Exorcism
Happiness
Hex-/Spell-Breaking

214

Love—Passion

Psychic Development
   and Growth

SAFFRON   FIRE   ☉

Commanding

Exorcism

Happiness

Hex-/Spell-Breaking

Psychic Development
   and Growth

SAGE   AIR   ♃

Cleansing

Consecration

Divination

Harmony and Balance

Peace

Protection

Psychic Development
   and Growth

Purification

Retention

Secrets

Strength

Wisdom

SANDALWOOD   WATER ☽

Harmony and Balance

Protection

Spirituality

Wisdom

**SANDALWOOD—
RED**   WATER ☽

Fidelity

Honesty

Love

Protection

SANDALWOOD   WATER ☽

Calming

Love—Aphrodisiac

Psychic Powers

Wishes

SASSAFRAS   FIRE   ♃

Compassion

Gentleness

Strength

SESAME   FIRE   ☉

Chakra—Base

Chakra—Heart

Love—Passion

Prosperity/Money

Uplifting

SNOWDROPS   AIR   ☿

Rejuvenation

Renewal

Spirituality

SPANISH MOSS EARTH ♄

Dispel Negativity

Protection

SPEARMINT   AIR   ♀

Clarity

Consecration

Happiness

Love

Mental Powers

Prosperity/Money

Protection

Renewal

Transformation

Uplifting

SPIKENARD   EARTH ♄

Anointing

Chakra—Heart

Commanding

Harmony and Balance

Health

Love—Fidelity

Protection—Psychic

SPRUCE   EARTH ♄

Love—Fertility

Protection

Protection—Psychic

Strength

STRAWBERRY   WATER ♀

Good Luck

Happiness

Love

SWEET PEA   WATER ♀

Attraction

Compelling

Courage

Devotion

Drawing

Love—Fidelity

Love—Friendship

Loyalty

Strength

SWEETGRASS   AIR   ♀

Attunement

Calling Spirits

Spirituality

TANGERINE   FIRE   ☉

Antidepressant

Calming

215

Magical Oils by Moonlight

Clarity
Inspiration
Protection
Protection—Defense

THYME   **AIR**   ♀

Clairvoyance
Compassion
Consecration
Contact Other Planes
Courage
Divination
Healing
Love
Psychic Development
  and Growth
Purification
Strength

TUBEROSE   **FIRE**   ♂

Centering
Character
Love
Love—Aphrodisiac
Protection   ☉

TULIP   **EARTH**   ♀

Earth Spirit
Love
Prosperity/Money
Protection

VALERIAN   **EARTH**   ☿

Exorcism
Harmony and Balance
Hex-/Spell-Breaking
Love
Love—Aphrodisiac
Overcome Opposition

Peace
Protection—Psychic

VANILLA   **WATER**   ♀

Mental Powers
Calming
Passion
Relaxing

VAN-VAN   **EARTH**   ♀

Clarity
Mental Powers
Power

VERBENA   **EARTH**   ♀

Calming
Concentration
Hex-/Spell-Breaking
Peace
Prosperity/Money
Protection
Purification

VERVAIN   **EARTH**   ♀

Consecration
Creativity
Inspiration
Knowledge
Material Objects
Nightmares
Prosperity/Money
Protection
Success
Transformation

VETIVERT   **EARTH**   ♀

Commanding
Good Luck
Grounding

Hex-/Spell-Breaking
Increase Power of Spells
Love
Love—Aphrodisiac
Prosperity/Money
Protection—Psychic
Regeneration
Strength

VIOLET   **WATER**   ♀

Beauty
Chakra—Throat
Fidelity
Good Luck
Happiness
Healing
Honesty
Modesty
Passion
Peace
Protection
Reuniting
Transformation
Wishes

WALNUT   **FIRE**   ☉

Wishes

WATER LILY   **WATER**   ☽

Anti-Aphrodisiac
Good Luck
Protection
Psychic Powers
Release
Renewal

WINTERGREEN   **EARTH**   ☿

Healing
Hex-/Spell-Breaking

Memory
Protection

WISTERIA   **AIR**   ♀

Contact Other Planes
Divine Intervention
Gentleness
Inspiration
Knowledge
Protection
Psychic Development
  and Growth
Wishes

WORMWOOD   **FIRE**   ♂

Clairvoyance
Contact Other Planes
Determination
Divination
Divine Intervention

Hex-/Spell-Breaking
Love—Aphrodisiac
Overcome Opposition
Protection
Psychic Development
  and Growth
Psychic Powers
Transformation

YERBA SANTA   **EARTH**   ♄

Exorcism
Hex-/Spell-Breaking
Protection
Psychic Development
  and Growth
Strength

YLANG-YLANG   **WATER**   ♀

Calming
Harmony and Balance

Love
Love—Aphrodisiac
Magnetic to Higher
  Vibrations
Peace
Relaxing
Strengthen Spirit

YULA   **WATER**   ♆

Connection to Higher
  Energies
Protection

ZULA-ZULA   **AIR**   ♃

Celestial
Magnetic to Higher
  Vibrations
Spirituality

Index

About the Author

Maya Heath is an internationally known artist and author who has appeared on television and radio, and has traveled the country working with the New Age community as well as the Pagan Witchcraft community. She has been a featured speaker at metaphysical fairs and expos as well as Pagan gatherings such as Craftwise in Connecticut, the Heartland Pagan Festival in Kansas City, and the Phoenix Festivals in Florida. She has given classes on wish spells and divination, energy work and healing, and stone and crystal work. Her books include *The Egyptian Oracle*; *Energies: A Book of Basics*; *Ceridwen's Book of Incense, Oils and Candles*; and *The Book of Stones and Metals*. Among her many artistic endeavors, she designs and markets metaphysical and alternative spirituality jewelry under the name Dragonscale Jewelry. When not traveling, she lives with her partner and their extended family, including three lazy cats, just outside of Orlando, Florida.